C000128142

By-Paths of Bible Knowledge.

V.

GALILEE IN THE TIME OF CHRIST.

BY

REV. SELAH MERRILL, D.D.,

Author of ' East of the Jordan,' &c.

WITH A MAP OF GALILEE.

THIRD Epnιῳ.

THE RELIGIOUS TRACT SOCIETY,
56 PATERNOSTER ROW, 65 ST. PAUL'S CHURCHYARD,
AND 164 PICCADILLY.

1891

CONTENTS.

	PAGE
PREFACE	7
SECTION	
I.—INTRODUCTORY	9
II.—HOW THE COUNTRY WAS GOVERNED, FROM B.C. 47 TO A.D. 66	12
III.—THE NAMES 'GALILEE,' AND 'GALILEE OF THE GENTILES'	15
IV.—EXTENT OF GALILEE, AND THE NUMBER OF INHABITANTS TO A SQUARE MILE . .	17
V.—GALILEE A REGION OF GREAT NATURAL FERTILITY AND RICHNESS	22
VI.—THE WATERS OF GALILEE	28
VII.—THE PLAIN OF GENNESARETH . . .	33
VIII.—AGRICULTURAL PRODUCTIONS AND MANUFACTURES	35
IX.—THE SEA OF GALILEE A FOCUS OF LIFE AND ACTIVITY	46
X.—THE NOTED CITIES AND TOWNS OF GALILEE	48
XI.—JOSEPHUS' STATEMENT AS TO THE NUMBER OF TOWNS AND INHABITANTS PROBABLY CORRECT	62

SECTION   PAGE

XII.—CHARACTER OF THE GALILEANS . . 68

XIII.—RELIGION, EDUCATION, AND MORALS AMONG THE GALILEANS 82

XIV.—THE POETICAL TALENT FINELY DEVELOPED AMONG THE GALILEANS 93

XV.—THE PROPHETS, JUDGES, AND OTHER FAMOUS MEN OF GALILEE 94

XVI.—THE WEALTH AND MATERIAL PROSPERITY OF THE PROVINCE 98

XVII.—WAS GALILEE REGARDED WITH CONTEMPT BY THE PEOPLE OF JERUSALEM, AS IS SO OFTEN ALLEGED? 104

XVIII.—NAZARETH, ITS CHARACTER AND PROBABLE SIZE; ORIGIN OF THE NAME; NOT SO ISOLATED AS IS SUPPOSED 113

XIX.—SUMMARY OF RESULTS GALILEE PROVIDENTIALLY FITTED FOR THE FIRST RECEPTION OF CHRIST AND HIS GOSPEL . . . 120

LIST OF AUTHORITIES QUOTED 123

INDEX 127

PREFACE.

————••————

THE object of this work is to represent Galilee as it was in the time of our Lord. To do this will be, the author feels, a special service to many who are desirous of learning all that can be known of the earthly life of Christ. In fairness to the reader, it should be stated that the substance of this volume appeared as an Essay in 1874, which met with a very flattering reception in England, Germany, and America. The text for the present edition has been thoroughly revised and partly re-written. It is published now in the hope that the perusal of these pages will lead some minds to appreciate more forcibly than they have ever done before that the country where the Master appeared was Divinely chosen for that purpose, and that its natural features symbolise in a great degree both the beauty and the strength of the Christian Religion.

GALILEE IN THE TIME OF CHRIST.

—◆—

I.

INTRODUCTORY.

THE fact is sometimes overlooked that a Divine
revelation implies history, and that history implies locality. Hence a familiar acquaintance with its
locality and history would seem to be necessary, if one
would fully appreciate and understand such a revelation,
whether it comprises a series of events extending over
many centuries, or is embodied in the person and life of
a single individual. It may not be, therefore, a rash
conclusion that our Lord meant to call attention to
this fact by His constant reference to the natural objects
about Him. This interesting characteristic of His teaching is indicative of one of the prominent methods by
which His life is to be approached. The infinite beauty
of His character will not appear in its clearest light if
we study Him from the spiritual side alone. We seem
to draw near to Him in the flesh in proportion as we
become acquainted with the country where He lived,
the race to which He belonged, and the scenes and
events amid which He grew up to manhood.

When we actually turn to books, commentaries, and other sources of information concerning the home of our Lord, we are introduced at once to a poverty-stricken land and to a degraded peoplè. The province is spoken of as having been, at that period, one of the most 'obscure' and 'despised' of the Roman empire, and Nazareth has the misfortune of being represented as then an 'insignificant village,' whose inhabitants were 'ignorant' and even 'immoral.' Such is, perhaps, the general impression of Galilee; but it is very far from the truth. The writers of the Gospels invariably speak of Nazareth as a 'city,' πόλις, and in no case do they call it a 'village,' κώμη; and it is quite probable that its population amounted to fifteen thousand or twenty thousand souls. As to the province itself, it was in Christ's time one of the gardens of the world—well watered, exceedingly fertile, thoroughly cultivated, and covered with a dense population.

The object of the present work is sufficiently indicated by its title. It may be said, however, that the subject could hardly be confined to the dates which bound the life of Christ. We must be allowed to illustrate our subject to some extent, at least, both by what preceded this period,—say, during the life of Herod the Great,—and by what followed it, even to the destruction of Jerusalem by Titus. Still, our sole purpose is to set forth Galilee as it was during the life of our Lord.

The work now proposed has never, so far as we are aware, been thoroughly done; and almost the only attempts in this field are those of Hausrath and Keim.

But the former is very brief (hardly ten pages); and the latter, although a little fuller (about sixteen pages), does not pretend to exhaust the subject. We have patiently searched in every direction for facts which might illustrate this country at the time when 'Jesus went everywhere among its cities and villages, teaching and preaching the gospel of the kingdom.' But it will be seen that, instead of putting the statements of the Gospels foremost, we have kept them in reserve, and have sought to gather from all external sources those facts by which to light up the background against which the statements of the Gospels rest. We shall, at the close of the volume, give a brief notice of some of the principal books which have served us in our investigations.

The map prefixed to the book is reduced, by the kind permission of the Committee of the Palestine Exploration Fund, from their large scale map of Galilee.

II.

HOW THE COUNTRY WAS GOVERNED, FROM B.C. 47 TO A.D. 66.

IT will be necessary to give a brief outline of the manner in which Palestine was governed during the period now under consideration. In B.C. 47, Herod, then a young man twenty-five years of age, was appointed by his father, Antipater, military governor of Galilee, and his brother, Phasaelus, military governor of Judæa. In B.C. 41, Phasaëlus and Herod were appointed by Antony tetrarchs of Judæa, i.e. of the whole province west of the Jordan. In B.C. 40, Phasaëlus was taken prisoner by the Parthians, who had invaded Syria, sweeping the country as far south as Jerusalem ; and, rather than suffer indignities and cruelties from his barbarian enemies, he put an end to his own life even while his hands were bound. The same year Herod was declared king of Judæa by the Roman Senate, although it was not until three years later, or in B.C. 37, that he became master of his kingdom, and entered upon his reign. He died in Jericho, April 1, B.C. 4, at the age of seventy. The same year Archelaus, Herod's son, was appointed by Augustus ethnarch of Judæa, Samaria, and Idumæa. At the same time Augustus appointed Herod Antipas, Archelaus's brother, tetrarch of Peræa and Galilee, and Herod Philip, half-brother of Archelaus and Antipas, tetrarch of Batanæa, Trachonitis, Auranitis, Paneas, and Gaulanitis.   Luke in his Gospel[1], speaking in a general way, mentions only Trachonitis and Ituræa.   In A.D. 6, Archelaus was banished by Augustus, and Judæa came directly under the Romans.   In A.D. 33, Herod Philip died, and was buried in Eastern Bethsaida.   In A.D. 32, Herod Antipas was banished, his wife Herodias going with him into exile.   In A.D. 37, Herod Agrippa I., grandson of Herod the Great, was by the emperor Caligula made 'king' of Trachonitis, i.e. of the region which had been Herod Philip's tetrarchy.   In A.D. 41, Claudius added to his dominions Judæa and Samaria, with Abilene, i.e. the tetrarchy of Lysanias, and the parts about Libanus. In A.D. 44, King Agrippa persecuted the Christians, beheaded James the brother of John, and arrested Peter.   The same year, however, Agrippa died in a strange manner at Cæsarea on the sea-coast.   The account of his violent disease and sudden painful death is given by Josephus[2], and also in the twelfth chapter of the Acts.   In the latter place will be found the details of Peter's miraculous escape from his imprisonment. Agrippa had been king of Judæa from A.D. 41 to 44. Judæa came again directly under the Romans.   In A.D. 53, Agrippa II., son of the former, was by Claudius made 'king' of Herod Philip's tetrarchy—Trachonitis, Auranitis, Gaulanitis, Batanæa, and Abilene.   In A.D. 55, Agrippa II. received from Nero, in addition to the country already under his dominion, the cities of Tiberias and Tarichæa in Galilee, and Julias, together

---

[1] Luke iii. 1.   [2] *Ant.*, XIX. viii. 2.

with fourteen villages about it, and Abila, all of which
were in Peræa.   In A.D. 60, he heard Paul's defence at
Cæsarea, the place just mentioned, where his father had
died.   He rendered great service to Vespasian during
the Jewish war, taking sides against his country.

Some points to be remembered as of special importance are the following :—1. That Herod Antipas was
the only civil ruler to whom Christ was subject.   2. The
very long reign of Herod Antipas.   3. The long reign
of the mild and prosperous ruler Herod Philip.   4. That
Judæa from A.D. 6 to A.D. 66, the time of the revolution,
was governed by Roman officials, with the exception of
from A.D. 41 to A.D. 44, when Herod Agrippa I. was
king.   The fact that Judæa was thus governed will
hereafter be seen to be of great importance in estimating
the contrast between affairs there and those in Galilee
during the same period.

III.

THE NAMES 'GALILEE,' AND 'GALILEE OF THE GENTILES.'

IT does not belong to the limits of the present work to show how this province came to be called Galilee. The origin of the word thus applied is, indeed, obscure. It is a word of pretty frequent occurrence in the Hebrew Bible, and has a variety of meanings, among which are *circuit* or *district*. But as Philistia, the Jordan valley, the wild and savage region west of the Dead Sea, and the northern part of the country, are thus designated, it is evident that no particular section could originally have been intended by it. The significance of the phrase in Isa. ix. 1, 'Galilee of the nations,' or, as it is rendered in the English version of Matt. iv. 15, 'Galilee of the Gentiles,' is by no means clear, so far as referring to any region that was defined by fixed geographical limits. We are convinced that there is no ground for identifying 'Galilee of the Gentiles,' as Jahn[1] and some other writers have done, with what was known in later times as 'Upper Galilee.' Further, the location of the 'twenty cities in the land of Galilee[2],' given by Solomon to Hiram, is also unknown. Ewald calls these cities 'small,' and Ritter refers to them as 'small and unimportant places probably;' whereas the Hebrew gives

---

[1] *Bib. Arch.*, § 25, p. 31.   [2] 1 Kings ix. 11.

no hint of that kind whatever. In our opinion they were heathen cities subject to Solomon; for the Jewish king would hardly have given away twenty cities occupied by his own people, unless he had been brought into great financial straits, which was not the case And although Strabo states that 'the inhabitants of Galilee, of the Plain of Jericho, and of the territories of Philadelphia and Samaria,' were composed of 'mixed tribes of Egyptians, Arabians, and Phœnicians,' we feel justified in claiming that the cities of both Upper and Lower Galilee were, with a very few exceptions, occupied by a Jewish population.

'Cabul,' the word used by Hiram, has never been satisfactorily explained, so far as the special meaning which he intended to give it is concerned. Of the passage in 1 Kings ix. 13, explanations may be found in the lexicons of Gesenius and Furst, also in Josephus[1] and in Ewald; Ewald rejects altogether that of Josephus. For a reason why Solomon gave these cities to Hiram, see Ewald's *History of Israel*, III., p. 292. In connection with Isa. ix. 1, the passage in 1 Mac. v. 15 *et seq.* should be compared, and in Keim, I., p. 308, will be found some hints on the name 'Galilee.'

---

[1] *Ant.*, VIII. v. 3.

IV.

EXTENT OF GALILEE, AND THE NUMBER OF INHABITANTS TO A SQUARE MILE.

GALILEE embraced the northern portion of the country west of the Jordan, covering in the main the territory of the four tribes, Asher, Naphtali, Zebulun, and Issachar. The boundaries of these tribes are given definitely enough in Josh. xix., but it is impossible to trace them now, because the places mentioned as marking the boundaries have not, with very few exceptions, been identified. For the same reason the boundary line of this province, so explicitly laid down by Josephus[1], is lost to us, as well as the line dividing between what in his day were known as 'Upper' and 'Lower' Galilee. When the division of the country took place among the four tribes just referred to, there were, in all, sixty-nine cities mentioned by name. For the most part their sites are unknown. In Josephus' time this province numbered two hundred and four cities and villages, of which the names of about forty are given by him. Of this number not more than ten can be located with any great degree of certainty; perhaps as many more could be located approximately; while the rest remain unidentified. Ritter called this region, 'a true *terra incognita.*'

The very best maps of Galilee hitherto have erred in

---

[1] *Wars,* III. iii. 1.

B

trying to tell more than is absolutely known of that country. Their authors have been actuated by the commendable desire to place before readers and students the information they needed ; but in doing so they have sometimes helped to give the authority of tradition to a certain site which modern researches have shown cannot be the true one.

The accurate and reliable map published by the Palestine Exploration Fund is our best authority for the present topography of the country : but with this important help it is still impossible to do more than indicate the general outline of the province as it was known twenty or thirty centuries ago. The sixty-nine cities of Joshua, or the forty cities and villages mentioned by Josephus, have not yet been identified, although within recent years a few sites have been recovered and added to the list of those previously known. In Upper Galilee sixteen of the nineteen cities of Naphtali were 'fortified' (עָרֵי מִבְצָר, *'arēī mibhtzar*)[1]. After all the careful and successful explorations that have been made hitherto in this region, it still remains, beyond doubt, a rich field for research. Relics, foundation stones, and ancient sites are waiting to be brought to light on the hill-summits of Naphtali, as well as in the territory of the other tribes that occupied the northern province of Palestine. Fortunately, the object we now have in view can be accomplished without knowing definitely the location of those cities and towns which once made this region a centre of life and prosperity.

---

[1] Josh. xix 35.

During the period under consideration the limits of Galilee may have varied somewhat with the changes in its own and neighbouring rulers. Carmel once belonged to it, but was, in Josephus' time, under the control of the Tyrians. The Lake of Tiberias and the River Jordan may at one period have formed the eastern boundary; but the Talmud reckons Gamala, which was situated on the east of the lake, together with the region above Gadara and Cæsarea Philippi, as belonging to Galilee [1]. Graetz refers to a passage in the Talmud which makes Jotapata and Gischala mark the north or north-western boundary. Lightfoot gives some very good reasons why Peræa, or a portion of it, might in Christ's time have been included under the general name of 'Galilee.' This would harmonise with the statement just given from Neubauer respecting the region about Gadara.

The division of Galilee into 'upper' and 'lower,' familiar to us from Josephus, is recognised by the Talmud, which has, however, a division peculiar to itself, as follows : 'Galilee contains the upper, the lower, and the valley. Thus the country above Kefr Chananyah, where the sycamore is not found, is called Upper Galilee ; the country below Kefr Chananyah, where the sycamore flourishes, is called Lower Galilee ; while the valley is the district of Tiberias [2].'

Where the boundaries remain so indefinite it is impossible, of course, to give the exact extent of its territory. The whole territory of Palestine, including that of the trans-Jordanic tribes, has been estimated at about 11,000

[1] Neubauer, pp. 178, 236, 242.   [2] Shebiith ix. 2.

square miles [1]. From the recent surveys the country
west of the Jordan is found to contain 6,000 square
miles, and the country east of the Jordan, reckoning that
which properly belongs to Eastern Palestine, contains
about the same number. Of the territory west of the
Jordan, it is safe to say that Galilee occupied about
one-third—perhaps a small third. Mr. Phillott's estimate, in the article 'Census,' just referred to, is without doubt altogether too low, as he allows only 930
square miles to Galilee. On the other hand, Keim's
estimate may be too high, as he allows to it about 2,000
square miles.

But the limits of the province have seemed to many
persons too narrow for the number of inhabitants it is
purported to have contained. The question has been
asked how three millions or more people could have
been crowded into such a space, and supported there in
comfort, and often in luxury. The problem, however,
may not have been such a difficult one as it appears to
those who have given the matter but little consideration.
About the Sea of Galilee, only thirteen miles long by
seven broad, there were ten or more flourishing cities
and towns. This seems improbable , but the fact is
established beyond dispute. Among illustrative facts
bearing upon this point we may mention that the island
of Malta had, in 1849, a population of 1,182 to the
square mile. The county of Lancashire had 1,064, and
that of Middlesex 6,683 inhabitants to the square mile.
The island of Barbadoes, with an area of about 166
square miles, without any large towns, without manu-

[1] Smith's *Bible Dict.*, art. 'Census.'

factures of any description, a purely agricultural colony, supports a population of 180,000 souls, or over 1,084 to the square mile. Considering the fact that Galilee had a number of large cities, and that the whole province was dotted with important towns, its 2,000 square miles may have supported 3,000,000 inhabitants.

V.

GALILEE A REGION OF GREAT NATURAL FERTILITY AND RICHNESS.

THE province to which our attention is now called was by no means the least favoured, nor the least important portion of the Holy Land. On account of its astonishing fruitfulness, its many resources, and its hardy population, it ranked next to Jerusalem in importance; 'it was the bulwark of Jerusalem' in more senses than one. The Gospels, in those portions of them which relate to Galilee, place it in an exceeding fertile region, whose surface was covered with 'cities and villages' which were crowded with a dense population, and full of energy and life. Most travellers in that country, and those writers who have studied its physical characteristics, represent it as being of great natural fertility and beauty, remarkably diversified by mountain and hill, valley and plain, springs, rivers, and lakes, while its climate is the 'nearest possible approach to a perpetual spring.' Josephus, Tacitus, the Babylonian Talmud (A.D. 500), Antoninus Martyr (A.D. 600), and almost any number of authorities since the time of the latter, have been unanimous in praising the natural beauties and resources of Galilee. Here is 'the most fertile soil in all Palestine.' To one its beautiful lake is 'the eye of Galilee.' The Rabbis compared the lake to 'gliding waters.' 'The shores of Tiberias formed one of the gardens of the world.' To another the Plain of Gennesareth is 'the unparalleled garden of God.' The Rabbis testify again that the shores of the lake were 'covered with cities, villages, and market-places.' Pliny speaks of the 'Lake of Genesara' as 'skirted by pleasant towns,' among which he mentions Julias, Hippos, Tarichæa, and Tiberias. The Hebrews said: 'The land of Naphtali is everywhere covered with fruitful fields and vines; and the fruits of this region are renowned for their wonderful sweetness[1].' 'If Nature could influence mind, if it could create genius, Naphtali would be the land of poets.' 'For sixteen miles about Sepphoris the region was fertile, flowing with milk and honey.' 'Galilee is a land of water-brooks, abounding in timber, fertile and beautiful.' The words of the dying lawgiver in regard to the four tribes which settled in this section lead us to expect that they were to occupy a region of great richness and beauty, or, in other words, applying to the territory what was said of the people, a land 'full with the blessing of Jehovah[2].' All that we know of the country since confirms the impression given by Moses. Renan, with glowing language, speaks of this region as 'a country very green, and full of shade and pleasantness, the true country of the Canticle of Canticles and of the songs of the well-beloved.'

In addition to these testimonies the statements of Josephus are of special importance, since, as military governor of the province, he knew thoroughly its cha-

[1] Neubauer (p. 180) gives references to Tal. Bab., Megilla 6a, and Berakoth 44 a.   [2] Deut. xxxiii. 23.

racteristics and resources. Of the country in general he says :—'It is throughout rich in soil and pasturage, producing every variety of tree, and inviting by its productiveness even those who have the least inclination for agriculture ; it is everywhere tilled, no part allowed to lie idle, and everywhere productive[1].'   And he speaks of the Plain of Gennesareth as 'admirable both for its natural properties and its beauty.'   'Such is the fertility of the soil that it rejects no plant, and accordingly all are here cultivated by the husbandman ; for so genial is the air that it suits every variety.   The walnut, which delights beyond other trees in a wintry climate, grows here luxuriantly, together with the palm-tree, which is nourished by heat ; and near to these are figs and olives, to which a milder atmosphere has been assigned.   One might style this an ambitious effort of Nature, doing violence to herself in bringing together plants of discordant habits, and an admirable rivalry of the seasons, each, as it were, asserting her right to the soil ; for it not only possesses the extraordinary virtue of nourishing fruits of opposite climes, but also maintains a continual supply of them   Thus it produces those most royal of all, the grape and the fig, during ten months, without intermission, while the other varieties ripen the year round.'   He goes on to speak of 'the genial temperature of the air,' of the plain being 'irrigated by a highly fertilising spring,' and of the fish, similar to those found in the Lake of Alexandria.

There can be no doubt that this land had been remarkably favoured by Nature.   The Hebrew phrase,

[1] *Wars*, III. iii. 2, 3.

'a land flowing with milk and honey,' might best express the exceeding fertility and richness of Galilee at the time of Christ. The capabilities of the soil were perhaps fully developed by skilful labour. The industrious farmers devoted their chief attention to the crops best adapted to their soil, and which at the same time found the readiest market ; hence, in many cases, meadow and pasture land were turned into tillage, because the cultivation of grain and fruits was found to be more profitable than the raising of cattle. The rich fields were sometimes so parcelled out that the plough could no longer be employed, and the soil must be turned up with the spade. Yet in the open fields where the plough was used the workmen prided themselves on being able to turn and lay a furrow with skill [1], which would never have been attempted in the stony fields of Judæa.

With such a soil, and under such thorough cultivation, it is not surprising that the country became a paradise in beauty. All the trees and fruits of Palestine flourished here to perfection. It was even asked why the fruits of Gennesareth were not found in Jerusalem at the time of the feasts, and the reply was made, ' so that no one may be tempted to come to the feasts merely for the sake of enjoying those fruits.' Here were found all the productions which made Italy rich and beautiful, with the additional advantage that here also 'the palm and the balm-tree flourished in great luxuriance ;' in the eyes of the Romans ' these palm groves were beautiful and lofty.' In a word, forests in many cases covered its

[1] Luke ix. 62 ; xvi. 3.

mountains and hills, while its uplands, gentle slopes and broader valleys, were rich in pastures, meadows, cultivated fields, vineyards, olive-groves, and fruit trees of every kind.   Here in this 'garden that has no end,' flourished the vine, the olive, and the fig, the oak, the hardy walnut, the terebinth, and the hot-blooded palm; the cedar, cypress, and balsam; the fir-tree, the pine, and sycamore; the bay-tree, the myrtle, the almond, the pomegranate, the citron, and the beautiful oleander. These, with still many other forest, fruit, and flowering trees, and shrubs, and aromatic plants, together with grains and fruits, to which should be added an infinite profusion of flowers, made up that wonderful variety of natural productions which adorned and enriched the region where was the home of Jesus.

The two last paragraphs have been left as they were originally written in 1873, partly for the reason that, when this work first appeared as an essay, the statements in this section were thought by some persons to be very much overdrawn; but the Rev. Dr Zeller, who spent eighteen years as a missionary in Nazareth, and whose knowledge of the region is extensive and intimate, examined the work, and his first criticism was that the facts with regard to the natural fertility of Galilee had been *underrated*.   It is hardly necessary to add any-thing, from still other sources, to this important and decisive testimony.   But it should be remembered that Dr. Zeller bases his conclusion upon his acquaintance with the country in its decay.

The characteristic now referred to is one for which Galilee was always celebrated.   In Solomon's time this region furnished many of the luxuries required for the table and the palace of the king.   Of the twelve commissariat officers who supplied for the royal establishment enormous quantities of fine flour, meal and barley, and great numbers of fat oxen, pasture-fed oxen, sheep, harts, roebucks, fallow-deer, and fatted fowl[1], four, and perhaps five, were stationed within the limits of the province we are now considering.   Hence, not only the abundance, but the great variety of its productions may properly be inferred.

Furthermore with regard to forests, it is probable that in ancient times this was a well-wooded country. Scattered notices in the Old Testament justify this conclusion, and, for a single later testimony, to which many more examples might be added, we may refer to Josephus[2], where he speaks of the hills about Jotapata being stripped of timber to be used in carrying on the siege of that place.   The soil of Galilee is well adapted to forest culture, and were proper care taken, the region might, in a generation or two, be enriched by a noble growth of oak and other trees.

It is hardly within the limits proposed to ourselves to speak of the condition of the country in our own time : yet we may call attention to the works of Tobler, Ritter, Arnaud, and Tristram, where will be found brief notices of some of the present productions of this region, such as wheat, barley, millet, pulse, indigo, rice, sugar-cane, oranges, the cherry, pear, and apricot, the mulberry, and still other grains, fruits, shrubs, and plants, including tobacco.

[1] 1 Kings iv. 22, 23.   [2] *Wars*, III. vii. 8.

VI.

THE WATERS OF GALILEE.

GALILEE was a well-watered country. The words of promise spoken to the Hebrews in regard to the land which they were to enter, 'a land of brooks of water, of fountains, and depths that spring out of valleys and hills[1],' would be truer of Galilee than of any other section. The lakes of this province, with their blue, transparent waters, contribute not a little to the charming beauty of the landscapes. The water of Lake Merom is sweet, as is also that of Lake Tiberias, and crystal clear. The Rabbis find it difficult to praise enough their beautiful lake, which was justly the pride of their whole land. They speak, in a phrase already quoted, of its 'gracefully flowing' or 'gliding waters.' Jehovah, they said, had created seven seas, and of these He had chosen the Sea of Gennesareth as His special delight. The names of these seas are given as the Great Sea, or the Mediterranean; the Sea of Tiberias, which was also known to them as Genusar; the Sea of Samecho, known in Josephus as Semechonitis; the Salt Sea, or the Sea of Sodom; the Sea of Hultha; the Sea of Shelhath, or Sheliyath; and the Sea of Apamia.

In the view of the Christian, in a far higher sense than

[1] Deut. viii. 7.

was thought of by the Rabbis, God has indeed chosen the Sea of Galilee, and blessed it beyond all other seas of the earth.

The Jordan, the only stream in Palestine deserving the name of 'river,' with its 'sources,' its 'floods,' and its remarkably winding course, belonged, at least in its upper and finer half, to Galilee. Perhaps the Litany, where it bends from a southerly to a westerly course, touched upon the northern frontier of this province. Here belonged the Kishon, the famous 'river of battle,' called in the song of Deborah and Barak 'that ancient river.' It took its rise near the foot of Tabor, went in a winding course across the plain of Esdraelon, and entered the Bay of Acre, near the foot of Carmel. A principal feeder of this stream came from Gilboa and Engannim. It received 'the waters of Megiddo,' not far from the town of the same name. When the Kishon was at its height, it would be, partly on account of its quicksands, as impassable as the ocean itself to a retreating army. The river Belus should also be mentioned, which entered the sea near Acre, and from the fine sand of whose bed the Phœnicians, according to tradition, first made glass. The present name of the stream with which so important a fact is connected, is Nahr N'aman; but we are not so certain as to what name it bore in the early Hebrew history. In Josh. xix. 26 we find a Shihor Libnath mentioned, which has been thought to be identical with the river Belus of Josephus and Pliny. But this is doubted by so eminent a scholar as Mr. George Grove, who even thinks that the Hebrew words do not refer to any river.

'No less than four springs pour forth their almost full-grown rivers through the plain' of Gennesareth. 'Beautiful springs, characteristic of the whole valley of the Jordan, are unusually numerous and copious along the western shore of the lake[1].' Half-an-hour north of the town of Tiberias are five or six profuse springs lying near together and called the 'cool fountains,' to distinguish them from the hot ones south of the city. Ritter speaks of 'the hundred brooks' that distribute their waters through the neighbourhood of Banias, 'carrying fertility everywhere.' Thomson speaks of 'the ample supply of water about Ayûn.' Six streams have been counted flowing into Lake Huleh from the mountains lying west of it,—the largest of which streams is from forty to fifty feet wide. The abundance of dew which falls about Tabor, remarked by Burckhardt, Robinson, and others, was of the utmost importance to vegetation in that immediate neighbourhood. The 'dew of Hermon' was long ago praised[2], and the rich vegetation of the surrounding region is largely due to this fructifying influence. The perpetual snow on Hermon proved no doubt an unspeakable blessing to the people of this province, freshening the atmosphere by day and cooling it by night. The snow was even carried to Tyre, Sidon, and Damascus as a luxury, and labourers sweltering in the hot harvest fields used it to cool the water which they drank[3]. No doubt Herod Antipas at his feasts in Tiberias enjoyed also from this very source the modern luxury of ice-water! Not only were ice and

---

[1] Stanley, *Sinai and Palestine*, p. 366.   [2] Ps. cxxxiii. 3.
[3] Prov. xxv 13; Jer. xviii. 14.

snow from the mountains used for the purpose now
indicated, but the inhabitants of this city had still another
method of making warm water cool and delightful. This
method was in use throughout the Jordan valley, and
especially in Jericho, where the heat was intense. Water
from the fountain, lake, or stream was put into earthen
jars, which were of a great variety of sizes according to
the needs of families or individuals, and these were
exposed to the air, generally in a sheltered place, and
where a draught was felt. In this manner it became
extremely cold even in the hottest weather, and was
regarded as one of the greatest comforts of life. In
ministering to the sick, and in entertaining weary
travellers, 'a cup of cold water' was not only refreshing,
it was more highly prized than a bag of gold.

The warm springs of this province are also to be
noticed : at Biram, Gadara, and Tiberias, of which those
at the last place were perhaps the most renowned.
'These three springs,' the Rabbis say, 'remained after
the Deluge.' The exact location of Biram is not known,
nor do the limits of this work permit us to describe the
remarkable springs at Gadara. There is a large cluster
of them near Tiberias. Some of these are hot, and
are called by the Rabbis 'the boiling waters.' The
supply of water in the largest is sufficient to turn the
wheels of mills. Pliny, referring to these springs, uses
the expression, 'which are so conducive to the restora-
tion of health,' as though their medicinal qualities were
widely known. Josephus reports that when he was
governor of Galilee, his enemy, John of Gischala, asked
him for 'permission to come down and use the hot

baths of Tiberias for the benefit of his health.' The permission was granted, although John really desired it as
an opportunity of carrying out his schemes of political
intrigue. We find a case where a certain famous Rabbi,
Joshua Ben Levi, being sick, bathed in these warm
springs, supporting himself meantime on the arm of a
friend. These springs were indeed one of the 'watering-
places' of that age and country, the delightful resort of
people of means, and were visited also with great benefit
by the feeble or sick of the land, on account of the heal-
ing properties of the waters. People were attracted
hither from Jerusalem and all other parts of the land;
and no doubt the city of Tiberias was by this means
greatly increased both in size and importance.

If, in a word, we think of the numberless brooks and
mountain torrents, the springs, besides the warm ones
already mentioned, the reservoirs, the aqueducts and
watercourses, remains of which exist about the Plain
of Gennesareth and elsewhere, the fountains, the cisterns,
and the wells, we have a land in which there was no
lack of water, and one surprisingly favoured in this
respect above Judæa.

VII.

THE PLAIN OF GENNESARETH.

SOME special notice ought to be taken of the Plain of Gennesareth, perhaps in fertility and beauty the gem of the East, as it certainly was the gem of Palestine. We have already quoted Josephus' glowing description of it. It must not be thought of as of great extent. Josephus makes it thirty stadia long by twenty broad : and Porter, in his *Handbook*, 'three miles long by one broad ;' but two miles and a half long by one broad is all that is allowed to it by recent explorers. Here Nature had lavished her tropical profusion and glory. Trees retained their foliage throughout the whole year, and during ten months of the year grapes and figs ripened. In this rank soil grew the finest wheat of the land.

Strabo mentions a sweet or aromatic rush or cane as growing here, that was highly prized. We find the 'tents of Gennesareth' referred to, and the explanation given that 'temporary shady bowers or small tents were made,' in which the people lodged who 'gathered the fruits of its noble gardens.' Still, its superior and delicious fruits were not found at Jerusalem at the feast, lest, as we have seen, some persons might attend them for the sake of enjoying these fruits alone. Ritter, borrowing a phrase from Hippocrates, says that its climate was a 'harmonious mingling of the seasons,'

C

and the Rabbis referring to it as being near Tiberias, affirmed that it possessed both 'gardens and paradises.' To make the name 'Gennesareth' suggestive of the richness of the soil, or of the sweetness of its fruits, several fanciful interpretations have been adopted, such as referring it to the Hebrew *kinnor*, 'a harp,' signifying, 'its fruit is sweet as the sound of a harp;' to *gan*, 'garden,' and *sar*, 'prince,' meaning 'garden of princes,' or to *gan* and *osher*, 'riches,' i.e. 'a garden rich in fertility and productions.' We are not obliged to accept these explanations, still they serve to indicate the high estimation in which this little plain has been held by those who have known something of its natural wealth and beauty.

VIII.

AGRICULTURAL PRODUCTIONS AND MANUFACTURES.

1. *Oil.*—Of the productions of this province, fish, wine, wheat, and oil occupy a foremost place. On account of the fine quality and great abundance of the latter, as well as because it was an important article of commerce with other nations, this product deserves our first attention. The dying lawgiver said of Asher: 'Let him dip his foot in oil[1].' In allusion to this phrase the Rabbis said: 'In Asher oil flows like a river.' 'It is easier,' they said, 'to raise a legion [i.e. a forest] of olive-trees in Galilee than to raise one child in Judæa[2].' Gischala was renowned for the abundance of its oil. Once, when oil was wanted at Laodicea, men were sent to Jerusalem and Tyre to purchase; but the quantity desired could be found only in Gischala, in Galilee. While Asher produced the most oil, Tekoa produced the best. Tekoa was called the *alpha* for oil, while Gischala occupied the third place in the country in regard to the quantity and quality of oil produced. Both Syrians and Phœnicians drew their supplies from this province, and the traffic in this commodity alone proved a source of wealth to the Galileans. Attention is called to a

---

[1] Deut. xxxiii. 24.   [2] Neubauer, p. 180.

certain period when oil was ten times as dear at Cæsarea
as at Gischala. Josephus shows that both demand and
supply were great, the selling price high, and the revenue
large. Of the business at Gischala, John, the rival of
Josephus, once had a monopoly. He seems to have
been a man of shrewdness and cunning, and not above
making use of the misfortunes of his countrymen for
his own pecuniary profit. The Jews at Cæsarea Philippi
were, it appears, under some kind of strict military
discipline, and having only a very limited amount of
pure oil, they were on the point of being compelled
to use that produced by the heathen, which would
have been 'a violation of their legal institutions.' By
representations of this kind and other entreaties, John
obtained permission of Josephus to remove to Cæsarea
the pure oil that was in Gischala. But, taking advantage
of the necessities of the people, which caused the difference in the price of this article as already alluded to,
'he realised, by this sinister procedure, a vast sum
of money.' In the other villages and towns of Upper
Galilee, as well as at Gischala, great quantities of oil
were stored. Especially was this true of Jotapata, where
it was so abundant that it was used freely as a means of
defence when that place was besieged. Large quantities
of it were heated, 'for many were employed in the
work,' who 'poured it down upon the Romans on all
sides, hurling with it also their vessels glowing with
heat.' Being 'poured over those sheltered by their close-
locked shields,' 'the oil, insinuating itself readily under
their armour, spread over the whole body, from head
to foot, feeding, not less eagerly than flame, upon their

flesh.' 'And as they were cased in their helmets and breastplates, there was no extrication from the scalding fluid, and, leaping and writhing in anguish, they fell from the scaling-planks.' This novel but terrible and, as it proved, effective means of defence, 'soon scattered the ranks of the Romans,' who, 'scalded, rolled headlong from the ramparts in excruciating agony.'

By looking back to the days of Solomon, we may get a hint as to the productiveness of this country in the amount of agricultural products which this king furnished to Hiram as a yearly tribute.   This fact shows in what Solomon's country was rich, and what Hiram needed.   Besides immense quantities of wine, wheat, and barley, about two hundred thousand gallons of the best oil were sent to Hiram every year[1].   As the cities on the Phœnician coast advanced in wealth, and their commerce was extended, which was true as we approach the beginning of our era from the time of Solomon, the business of receiving supplies from Galilee was greatly enhanced.   Furthermore, in Christ's time oil was a common article in the treatment of the sick.   Herod the Great, in his last sickness, was almost killed by being plunged into a vessel of oil.   He was at this time at Jericho, and his body 'was racked with complicated sufferings.'   Hoping for relief, he visited the warm springs opposite Jericho, and there the physicians advised the treatment already mentioned.   'On their letting him down into a vessel filled with that fluid [warm oil], his eyes became relaxed, and he fell back suddenly as if

---

[1] 1 Kings v. 11 ; 2 Chron. ii. 10.

he were dead.' The cries of his attendants, however, roused him ; but he despaired of recovery, and returned to Jericho to die

In the affair of John's monopolising the oil trade of Gischala which Josephus condemns, Graetz takes decidedly the part of the former against the latter. Indeed, Graetz is throughout a bitter opponent of Josephus[1]. On p. 392 he says that the Galileans sold to the Phœnicians and Syrians their surplus oil, and received therefrom a large revenue. On p. 394 he states that the Galileans *did not* sell their surplus oil to their heathen neighbours, because it was forbidden to transport the means of life—oil and wine—out of the Jewish country.

The theory has been put forth by some, and stoutly maintained, that Christ was an Essene. But Christ, as we learn from Mark vi. 13, Luke x. 34, and many other passages, commended the use of oil in sickness, in anointing the body, and in every way according to the customs of the time ; while the Essenes renounced the use of oil altogether. Josephus says positively that 'they consider oil defiling ; and should any one accidentally come into contact with it, he wipes his body[2].' These facts go far towards settling the question whether Christ was an Essene.

2. *Certain Places noted for Particular Productions or Manufactured Articles.*—Our limits do not allow us to speak of the grain-production and other industries of this province with any great detail. We can only pass hastily in review the names of some of its prosperous towns, and speak of the manufactured articles or agri-

---

[1] Graetz, III. p 397.   [2] *Wars*, II. viii 3

cultural and other productions for which each was celebrated.   If the evidence on these points which we derive
from the Talmud does not all refer to the time of Christ,
or the first century (which cannot easily be decided), it
shows, at least, that in contrast with Judæa, Galilee had
decidedly the advantage in regard to agricultural products and industries of all kinds.

The figs, grapes, and other fruits of the Plain of
Gennesareth had a national reputation for their superior
quality.   The very name Gischala (*gush chaleb*, 'fat
soil') suggested the richness of that region.   The people
living there were mostly farmers.   The region about
Safed was noted for its fertility, as was also that about
Banias.   A portion of this northern district is still celebrated for its excellent wheat.   Notice is taken of the
fact that in this province but few small cattle were raised
(i.e. sheep and goats), because the rich land could be put
to a more profitable use.   These, however, were raised in
abundance in the waste regions of Judæa and Syria.
The heavy soil of the Plain of Jezreel produced superior
grain, which was fully equalled by that which grew in
the fertile fields of Gennesareth.   The wheat of Chorazin
and Capernaum was widely celebrated.   Bethshean, on
account of its fertility, was called the Gate of Paradise.
The Rabbis boast of the olives of that place, and also of
the fine and coarse linen garments which were there
manufactured.   Safed was celebrated for its honey;
Shikmonah for its pomegranates; Achabara for the
raising of pheasants.   Sigona furnished the best wine;
the region about Sepphoris was noted for the production
of grain and fruit.   Rabbi Jose, who lived in Galilee,

said . 'For sixteen miles on either side of Sepphoris
there flows milk and honey.'

Large quantities of grain were stored in the towns of
Upper Galilee, some of which, at the time referred to,
was probably the tribute belonging to the Roman
emperor. The same was true of certain places in Lower
Galilee.

Grain merchants congregated at Arabah. In the
siege of Jotapata there was no lack 'of all kinds of
provisions, except salt and water.' Magdala boasted of
three hundred shops where pigeons for the sacrifices
were sold. About this place the indigo plant flourished
then, as now, and the Talmud calls it 'the city of colour.'
More literally, one portion of the city was called 'the
tower of dyers,' and here were eighty shops where fine
woollen cloth was made. Arbela, also, was celebrated
for the manufacture of cloth.

Abundance of flax was raised in Galilee, and the linen
fabrics made here by the women were of unusual fineness
and beauty. A peculiar kind of vessel was necessary for
preserving oil, and of the manufacture of this Galilee
seems to have had a monopoly. Kefr Chananyah and
Sichin (Asochis ?) were the most noted places for earthen
vessels and pots. 'The pots made at Sichin, as well as
those made at Kefr Chananyah, are well baked and
solid.' 'The clay used in their manufacture is the dark,
and not the white kind.' This was the principal business
of the inhabitants of these two towns, and the business
was lucrative. 'To come from selling pots in Kefr
Chananyah,' was a proverbial saying, equivalent to the
French proverb, 'To carry water to the river.'

As to these pots made from black clay, it is possible that certain fragments of ancient pottery recently dug up at Jerusalem have some connection with them, at least to the *kind of ware* alluded to.   In the Birket Israil certain curious vases were found, 'all of an extremely hard, massive, black ware, coated in three instances with a dark crimson glaze, perhaps produced by cinnabar[1].'

We may add that in some of the ancient mounds which exist in Palestine and about old ruins the *débris* is composed largely of broken pottery.   This is of many colours ; but while the red is the prevalent kind, in a few localities the black exists almost to the exclusion of every other variety.

Galilee must have been largely affected by the commerce and other business interests of Phœnicia. Twenty miles from the Mediterranean would, at almost any point, take one into the heart of Galilee ; and the inhabitants of these two sections, living in such close proximity to each other, were, no doubt, to a great extent, identical in their interests.   It was not a small matter for the Galileans to be thus situated at the very gates of the markets of the world.   The ships of the people who controlled so largely the trade and commerce of all civilised lands were at their very doors.   Strabo says of the people of Tyre, 'the great number and magnitude of their colonies and cities are proofs of their maritime skill and power.'

The purple dye of Tyre had a world-wide celebrity on account of the durability of its beautiful tints, and its

[1] *Recovery of Jerusalem*, p. 374.

manufacture proved a source of abundant wealth to the inhabitants of that city. Homer speaks of Sidon as 'abounding in works of brass,' and praises it for the drinking-vessels of gold and silver which its skilful workmen had made. From this city, even in his time, came the choicest works of art, and the most costly offerings to the gods were the product of its looms. Both these cities were crowded with glass-shops, dyeing and weaving establishments; and among their cunning workmen not the least important class were those who were celebrated for the engraving of precious stones[1].

The Phœnicians were renowned in ancient times for the manufacture of glass, and some of the specimens of their work that have been preserved are still the wonder of mankind. Here and elsewhere it was produced in such abundance that before the commencement of our era glass was in ordinary use for drinking vessels, and a glass bowl could be bought for a penny. On the other hand, so much skill had been devoted to its manufacture that elegant and costly articles were produced, and for a single pair of vases Nero paid a sum equal to four thousand five hundred pounds. It is a noticeable fact that Galilee's own (original) coast, near the river Belus, including the bed of that stream, furnished the sand for the glass-shops of the world. 'Numerous ships' came here to convey this sand to other ports, Tyre, Sidon, and Alexandria, where, for a long period, the most famous workshops of this kind existed. The supply was said to be inexhaustible.

[1] 2 Chron. ii. 7, 14.

In the matter of shipping, whether ship-building be thought of, or traffic upon the sea, Phœnicia surpassed all other nations. This fact made that people the connecting link between the civilisation of the East and the vast and unknown regions of the West. Their ships went to all parts of the world as then known; and news of remote peoples, conquests, and discoveries would be brought first to Phœnicia, and disseminated among themselves and their immediate neighbours.

The commerce and business of Phœnicia would bring wealth, and wealth would bring power and ease, and in time a luxurious mode of life, which could not fail to influence in some degree the people of the hill-country only a few miles away. Flax for its looms, timber for its ships, corn, wine, oil, wheat, barley, sheep and cattle to feed its inhabitants, as well as for export to other countries, would be largely furnished by its nearest neighbour, Galilee, which was especially favoured in the production of all these staple articles of consumption and merchandise[1].

3. *Fisheries of the Sea of Galilee.*—We have yet to speak of the fisheries of the Sea of Galilee. The sea abounded in fish of the choicest kinds. The southern portion of the lake, especially, was in the time of Christ one of the finest fishing-grounds in the world. Some varieties caught here were similar to those found in the Nile; while other varieties were peculiar to this lake alone.

Not only Tarichæa, but Bethsaida also (if it really

[1] See Acts xii. 20.

means, as some claim, 'house of fish'), and to these
Keim would add Chorazin, derived their names from
the business of fishing; and all the cities about the lake
sent forth their fishermen by hundreds over its surface.
Tarichæa was noted for its extensive fish factories.
Here fish were prepared and packed, and, it has
been inferred with some reason, shipped to all parts
of the country and to the different cities about the
Mediterranean. They were sought as luxuries in the
market-places of Jerusalem. This trade in fish had
enriched the citizens of Tarichæa; and people came
even from Jerusalem, especially just before the great
feasts, to fish in these waters, and thus provide means
of support for the millions who on those occasions
flocked to the Temple.

This fishing-ground was free to all, so long as one by
his nets, hooks, or other means of catching the fish did
not interfere with the passage of boats. By a common
law of the land, dating, as was supposed, from the time
of Joshua, this ground could not be monopolised.

In Christ's time the Jews distinguished sharply between clean and unclean fish. This is, no doubt, alluded
to in the phrase, 'They gathered the good into vessels,
but cast the bad away[1];' for if τὰ καλὰ in this passage
means those that are good and of choice quality, τὰ
σαπρὰ must mean the opposite, or those of inferior or
poor quality. Without violence to the passage, we may
say that this phrase indicates that the fish-merchants
about the lake and in the distant markets where these
fish were sent, demanded the choicest kinds. And the

[1] Matt. xiii. 48.

Gospels themselves furnish evidence enough to show that this business in Christ's time was extensive and profitable [1].

But it is, probably, next to impossible for us at the present day to appreciate the extent of this particular industry of the Sea of Galilee in the time of our Lord. The same may be said of this business in Egypt in ancient times, with regard to which the following facts are interesting, and, in a sense, illustrative of our subject. Wilkinson, partly on the statements of Herodotus and Diodorus, reports the annual income of the fisheries of Lake Mœris and its sluices which led to the Nile as £70,700, while at present the annual revenue from the fish of Lake Mœris is only about £102 [2].

[1] Matt. iv. 18, 21; Luke v. 2-10; John xxi. 1-11, and elsewhere.
[2] *Ancient Egyptians*, 2nd edit., III. p. 64.

IX

THE SEA OF GALILEE A FOCUS OF LIFE AND ACTIVITY.

A MERE glance at the life of the lake is all that we can devote to this topic, before we pass on to consider the cities lying about it and those that were scattered throughout the province. In those days the sea was covered with ships and boats, engaged either in fishing or traffic, or carrying travellers or parties of pleasure from shore to shore. 'Merchants come and go from Hippos to Tiberias.' Hippos was on the east side of the lake, and Tiberias on the west. Once, when Josephus planned a certain movement against Tiberias, which was to start by water from Tarichæa, he collected for the purpose at that point, apparently in a short time, two hundred and thirty ships from the vicinity of Tarichæa alone. He says in his *Life*, that 'the sight of the lake covered with these vessels struck the Tiberians with terror.' Later, when this city expected an attack from the Romans, the citizens got ready a great number of vessels, to which they might flee in case of a repulse. The day went against them, and they fled to their ships; in these they made a bold resistance, and cost the Romans a fierce and bloody struggle before they could be overcome. That is a bloody sea-fight in which from four to six thousand are slaughtered on one side alone, as was the case here, and not a 'sharp skirmish,' as one has termed this event. As all could hardly have perished, the number of Jews killed is a hint, at least, that the number of ships on the side of the Tarichæans was large. We are speaking of Tarichæa alone; but when we think of all the cities and towns by which the lake was surrounded, we can easily understand that in Christ's time its ships and boats were very numerous. The difference between ships and the small boats which are attached to them is clearly brought out in the Greek of John xxi. 3, 6, 8. The phrase in Josephus 'climbing up into their ships,' is a significant hint as to the size of some of their vessels. And as to the appearance of the lake then : 'when we add to the fishermen the crowd of ship-builders, the many boats of traffic, pleasure, and passage, we see that the whole basin must have been a focus of life and energy; the surface of the lake constantly dotted with the white sails of vessels flying before the mountain gusts, as the beach sparkled with the houses and palaces, the synagogues and temples of the Jewish or Roman inhabitants[1].'

[1] *Sinai and Palestine*, p. 367.

X.

THE NOTED CITIES AND TOWNS OF GALILEE.

IF now we turn to the cities and inhabitants of this
province, we shall find a country whose surface was
dotted with flourishing towns, and covered with a dense
population. From the Gospels themselves, we should
expect to find here numerous 'cities and villages,'
swarms of people, activity and energy, much wealth,
and in some cases even luxury.

Beginning with the Sea of Galilee, we find upon
its shores no less than nine cities, while numerous
large villages could be counted on the plains and
hillsides around. Not far from Tiberias lay Bethmaus,
where was a synagogue. About an hour's walk, or a
little more than that, below the baths of Tiberias lay
Tarichæa, where the fish business was, as we have seen,
extensively carried on. The lake reached to the walls
on two of its sides. Of the sea-fight there we have
already spoken At that time many thousands of the
inhabitants were slain : six thousand robust young men
were sent to Corinth to work on the canal which Nero
was cutting through the Isthmus there, and thirty
thousand more were sold as slaves. This place had
had a hard fortune; for in B.C. 51 Cassius took it,
and carried into slavery thirty thousand of its inhabi-

tants. It was called a larger place than Tiberias.
Josephus was brought there by sea (probably because
the distance was considerable, and because Tiberias
was unfriendly to him) the night after he was wounded
near Capernaum. From a passage in Josephus, where
he states that 'materials for rafts were abundant' and
'workmen were numerous,' we gather that one of the
important industries of the city was ship-building.

Near Tarichæa, and just below the point where the
Jordan leaves the lake, there was a splendid bridge
across the river, supported by ten piers, and thronged
by soldiers, citizens, and merchant-caravans from the
rich plains and cities of the Decapolis, which lay to
the east.

Three or four miles from the Jordan, after crossing it,
on the eastern shore of the lake, was situated a town
which some scholars are inclined to identify with
Hippos, an important city of the district ruled by
Herod Agrippa II., a place where he sometimes resided,
and one that obtained considerable notoriety in the
Jewish war. But a more probable supposition as to
the site of Hippos, and the one which, in consequence
of our recent investigations, we are inclined to favour, is
that it is identical with the modern Fik. Still further
northward along the shore last mentioned, was situate
Gamala, called *Camel*, from the peculiar shape or outline
of the hill on which it stood. It was a little south of
east from Tiberias, and its walls and towers commanded
a fine view of the lake below and of the country on
every side. The Talmud reckoned it as a city of
Galilee. Josephus did not overrate the character of

D

this place when he called it 'the strongest city in
that part.' It was noted likewise for the bravery of
its inhabitants. This fact, combined with its 'strong
natural defences,' enabled it to withstand a siege of
seven months from Agrippa II., after it had revolted
from the Romans. Vespasian at last led against it
three veteran and famous legions, the 5th, 10th, and
15th, but they were vigorously repulsed, Agrippa was
wounded, and Vespasian himself was once surrounded
by the enemy and in imminent danger of losing his
life. At length, however, the tide turned against the
Jews, the fortress was subdued, and the garrison and
citizens were terribly punished.

A short distance farther north, on the left, or south
bank, of what is now called Wâdy Semakh, was Gergesa,
near which was the scene of the demoniacs and the herd
of swine[1]. Passing on up the eastern side of the lake, to
about one mile above where the Jordan enters it, one
would reach the Eastern Bethsaida. Herod Philip, the
tetrarch, had transformed this place from a fisherman's
village into a beautiful and flourishing city, and given it
a royal name, Julias, in honour of Julia, the daughter
of Augustus; and here, in a magnificent and costly
tomb, which he built for himself, Philip was buried
A. D. 33. It was near this city that Christ fed the five
thousand with the five loaves and two fishes, and, after
sending the multitudes away, retired to the neighbouring
hill to pray[2]. From this place, after crossing the Jordan,
to Tiberias, our starting-point, the distance is only four,
or perhaps six, hours' ride; yet, within this limited space,

---

[1] Matt. viii. 28-34.   [2] Luke ix. 10-17.

along the north-western and western shore of the lake, were situated in the time of Christ no less than four flourishing cities or towns, namely: Chorazin, the Western Bethsaida, Capernaum, and Magdala. If, however, we may judge from the ruins existing at the present time, there were at least seven instead of four such towns within the distance here indicated. From this Western Bethsaida, which was a beautiful 'city,' πόλις, by the sea, three disciples were called— Philip, Andrew, and Peter, and this may also have been the home of Zebedee and his two sons, the apostles James and John. John calls it Bethsaida in Galilee, to distinguish it from the other[1]. It was intimately connected with many events in the life of Christ. The fine wheat-fields about Chorazin and Capernaum we have already noticed. To the names now given should be added another, that of Beth-Arbel, or Arbela, as it was also called in Christ's time, distant about one hour from Tiberias, and lying west of Magdala. It had been celebrated as a stronghold from the days of Hosea[2]. Josephus speaks of its fortified caves, which at many periods, but especially in the early days of Herod the Great, were the hiding-places of robbers. Its situation was important, as it commanded the road from Carmel, Ptolemais, and Southern Galilee to Damascus. In B.C. 39, after Herod was made king, he crushed these robbers by a bold and thorough stroke, perfectly characteristic of the man.

Magdala was also, as we have already seen, a flourishing city of this densely populated region; the

[1] John i. 44; xii. 21.   [2] Hosea x. 14.

name has been immortalised in every language of
Christendom as denoting the birth-place of Mary
Magdalene, or better, Mary of Magdala.   Chorazin,
Bethsaida, and Capernaum were those in which ' most '
of the Master's 'mighty works were done,' and which,
' because they repented not[1],' He felt it necessary to
' upbraid ' and denounce.   Capernaum was for nearly
three years the home of Jesus.   Here all the elements
of Christ's character were exhibited as in no other
place.   His own words throw much light on the
condition of the city at that time.   It was one of the
chief points on the great caravan route, already referred
to, leading from Egypt and the sea-coast to Damascus.
It had its custom-house, its numerous tax-gatherers, its
Roman garrison, its schools, and its costly synagogue[2].

Besides the places already mentioned as lying on
or near the shore of the lake, we have yet to speak
of Tiberias, on the west side, and which, probably,
surpassed any one of the others, both in political and
social importance (both Capernaum and Tarichæa may
have equalled if not surpassed Tiberias in *commercial*
importance), as well as in the richness and splendour
of its buildings.   With a decided Roman taste, Antipas
(B.C. 4–A.D. 39) had lavished upon it vast sums of
money to make it a perfect city.   Here, close by the
warm springs, and bathed by the blue waters of the
lake, this luxurious and worldly Herod, the murderer
of John the Baptist, had built magnificent Grecian
colonnades, Roman gates, splendid public buildings,
including his palace, and adorned the city with marble

[1] Matt. xi. 20–24.   [2] Luke iv. 31.

statues, and sought to appease the Jewish portion of the citizens, to whom these things were no doubt very distasteful, by building for them perhaps the finest synagogue in all the north, 'in whose colossal basilica during the period of the revolution the assemblies of the people were held.'   The Βουλή, or council of nobles, of Tiberias numbered in the time of the Jewish war six hundred members.   Previous to the building of Tiberias, Sepphoris had been the chief city of Galilee. Lewin thinks that Antipas built Tiberias a few years before Christ began His public ministry, about A.D. 27. There had been either a battle here, or else an old burying-ground, for the workmen came upon quantities of human bones, which made the place unclean to the stricter Jews.   It is supposed that Christ never visited this city; for which two reasons are suggested: 1, He may have shared in the feeling of the orthodox Jews; or, 2, He may have wished to avoid Antipas[1].   In the time of Agrippa II. Tiberias was degraded below Sepphoris, and on this account there must have been some feeling between the citizens of the two places. Vespasian did not dare approach Tiberias, which had been fortified by Josephus, with less than three legions of his best troops.   The old prejudice on account of the bones at last died out, and the Rabbis have a tradition as to how the city was made pure.   Sailors formed quite a class among its inhabitants.   The place was the scene of many important events in the Jewish war.

But from the Jordan to the sea-coast, scattered every-

[1] For the Jewish law violated in connection with these bones, see *Ant.*, XVIII. ii. 3.

where among the hills, were numerous towns and cities, many of which were of great importance; we may mention Gischala, Kadesh, Safed, Cæsarea Philippi (Paneas), Cana, Ramah, Gabara, Jotapata, Japha, Gabatha, Zabulon, Hazor, Rimmon, Nazareth, Tabor, Sepphoris; and in the south Bethshean (Scythopolis), and possibly Gadara. It must not be supposed that this list embraces all of even the important places of Galilee, for Josephus states that it had two hundred and four cities and villages, the smallest of which numbered about fifteen thousand inhabitants. Tarichæa had forty thousand, and Scythopolis about the same number. Japha was the largest 'village' in Galilee, and strongly fortified. Zabulon was one of the largest cities in the north, and built in elegant style. It was 'a town of admirable beauty,' and 'its houses were built on the model of those of Tyre, Sidon, and Berytus.' This remark of Josephus will be significant when we add the statement of Strabo, that the houses of Tyre were many stories in height, 'more even than at Rome,' where Augustus, to check the passion for erecting lofty dwellings, decreed that buildings along the public ways at least should not exceed seventy feet in height. From the language we are to infer that, remote from the streets, they were still higher, and, of course, in other respects their elegant or magnificent character would correspond. Jotapata was 'the strongest of the cities fortified by Josephus.' Mount Tabor was a stronghold. There was a fortress on it at least from B.C. 218 to A.D. 70, which, however, dated probably from the early history of the country. In B.C. 218 it was taken by Antiochus the

Great, and in B.C. 55 Alexander, son of Aristobulus, and rival of Antipater, the father of Herod the Great, rallied his forces at Mount Tabor, but was defeated by Gabinius, and ten thousand of his men (i.e. Jews) were slain. This beautiful and conspicuous natural object, with its walls, towers and roofs, may well have been the 'city set upon a hill.' Safed, because of its lofty situation, was visible from the shores of the Sea of Galilee. Later, Safed and Tiberias formed two of the four sacred cities of the Jews ; the two others were Hebron and Jerusalem. Sepphoris was of great importance. It was called 'the security of all Galilee.' Here were the public archives of the province, after they were removed from Tiberias in the time of Agrippa II., and here also was a royal magazine of arms. Some of these cities were built on the summits of hills, or, in other cases, on the brows of the mountains, and, when seen from afar, were compared to 'birds resting upon lofty nests.' Many of those places that were strongly fortified were celebrated for severe and bloody struggles during the Jewish war, and for the bravery of their inhabitants—fighting to the death for their country and homes.

Cæsarea Philippi deserves special notice. 'It was the famous seat of idol-worship for many ages.' Its present name, Banias, is a corruption of *Panes*, which commemorates the worship of the Greek god Pan. But the name Paneas is in turn but a corruption of the far more ancient name *Balinas*, which commemorates the worship here of Baal ten and perhaps fifteen centuries before the place was even known to the Greeks. The old inhabitants of the land could hardly have selected a more charming locality than this as a religious centre. On account of its scenery alone it had been a place of note from the earliest times. It has been spoken of as 'the finest spot in the Holy Land ;' far up among, or rather under, the hills, beneath Hermon's 'eternal tent of snow,' with its castles and palaces, its grotto-sanctuary of Pan, and its marble gods, with scenery both picturesque and grand,—it might well be esteemed as 'beautiful for situation.'

West and south of the town stretched the great Huleh Plain and the Lake which was known in earlier times as 'the waters of Merom,' whose shores were the scene of one of the greatest battles of Joshua's time, when the tribes of Northern Canaan massed their forces—warriors, horses and chariots—'even as the sand that is upon the sea-shore in multitude[1],' for a final and desperate conflict with the invader. Seven centuries later these shores were desolated by the conquering army of Tiglath Pileser, King of Assyria[2]. Two centuries before Christ (B.C. 198) a great battle was fought immediately before this town between Scopas, the general of Ptolemy Epiphanes, and Antiochus the Great, in which a large part of Scopas' army was destroyed. This battle is specially memorable and interesting in the annals of Palestine because in it elephants were extensively used, which must have caused terror to the people of Upper Galilee who either witnessed or engaged in the struggle.

The 'grotto-sanctuary' just referred to, was, as Josephus describes it, 'a very fine cave in a mountain, under which there is a great cavity in the earth, and the cavern

---

[1] Josh. xi. 4.   [2] 2 Kings xv. 29.

is abrupt, and prodigiously deep, and full of still water; over it hangs a vast mountain, and under the caverns arise the springs of the Jordan[1].' In the parallel passage in the *Wars*[2], he describes 'a yawning chasm' in the cave, 'which descends to an immeasurable depth, containing a vast collection of still water, hitherto found unfathomable by any length of line.' Herod the Great adorned this place, 'which was already a remarkable one,' still further, by the erection of a beautiful temple of white marble, which he dedicated to Augustus. Under Herod Philip the place was greatly enlarged, and it enjoyed perhaps its most flourishing period, although it retained its importance throughout the first century at least.

Eastward from the town, towards Damascus, ran one of the main highways of the country, which from the days of Abraham had been a favourite route for invading armies. By a law of the land, these roads were of such width that chariots could meet and pass each other without difficulty or danger. On the north side of this highway, three miles from Cæsarea Philippi, stood one of the strongest castles in Syria, from whose walls and towers the beholder could look down on the Lake and Plain, and up to the highlands of Galilee that rose beyond. The public road, after crossing the Plain, divided and led up over the hills in two directions, one branch going to Sidon and the other to Tyre. Both roads were guarded by castles situated at the most commanding points. That on the road to Tyre was in full view from that above Banias, and as in those days

---

[1] *Ant.*, XV. x. 3.   [2] I. xxi. 3.

means for signalling from point to point were well known, the soldiers in these two fortresses—in times of danger or in moments of victory—no doubt by this means communicated with each other across the great Plain below.

This place has borne in history no less than seven different names, although Cæsarea Philippi is the only one by which it is known in the New Testament,—called thus to distinguish it from its sister city on the sea-coast. About the commencement of our era it had likewise a variety of masters. It is a curious but interesting fact that in the year 36 B.C. this town, and the region about it, were owned by the fascinating but infamous Cleopatra, having been bestowed upon her by the infatuated Antony. After her death it was farmed out to Zenodorus, a petty ruler, who disgraced his office by his intrigues with the robbers of the desert. On his death, in B.C. 20, Herod the Great came into possession of it, by whom it was bequeathed to his son Herod Philip. He died in A.D. 33, when it reverted to the Emperor Tiberius, and was attached to the Roman province of Syria. Scarcely four years passed before it was given by Caligula, in A.D. 37, to Herod Agrippa I., who died in A.D. 44. This is the person called in Acts xii. 1, 'Herod the King,' who died, as there narrated, a terrible death at Cæsarea on the sea-coast. For nineteen years subsequent to his death it was under the dominion of the procurators Cuspius Fadus, Tiberius Alexander, and Cumanus. At last it was bestowed upon Herod Agrippa II. in A.D. 53, to whom it belonged during the Jewish war, or from A.D. 66 to A.D. 70.

In A.D. 67, after the destruction of Jotapata, and Galilee was practically subdued, King Agrippa II. invited Vespasian to Cæsarea Philippi, and entertained him, it is said, 'in the best manner his resources permitted.' Here the Roman general 'rested his troops for twenty days, and enjoyed himself in festivities, presenting thank-offerings to God for his success,' i.e. over the patriots of Galilee. This was in midsummer, and his son Titus was with him during this interval of relaxation from their work of conquest. Three years later, in A.D. 70, after Vespasian had gone to Rome, Titus, who had taken Jerusalem, went again to Cæsarea Philippi, and remained some time, exhibiting public spectacles of various kinds. Very many of the Jewish prisoners taken at Jerusalem were brought hither at this time, and destroyed in the most violent and cruel manner. 'Some were thrown to wild beasts, while others, in large bodies, were compelled to encounter one another in combat.'

These facts show, on the one hand, that this place possessed unusual attractions, while, on the other, these scenes and deeds of cruelty and blood, which the Romans enjoyed, and even looked upon as sport, only add to the chequered history of this ancient town, which has witnessed almost every variety of fortune that cities or men can experience.

The interest of these few historical facts, as connected with this place, will be greatly enhanced, it seems to us, when we consider that Cæsarea Philippi was visited by our Lord, and that one of the foot-hills of Hermon, overlooking the region as well as the town itself, was the scene of the Transfiguration. This single fact would

make it one of the most sacred localities in the Holy
Land.   It was here that Christ questioned His disciples
as to His own character · 'Whom do men say that I,
the Son of Man, am [1]?'   On the one hand, before their
eyes as they sat and spoke together, were the military
power of Rome and pagan idolatry in its most fascinating forms, and on the other Christ and His disciples, a
humble band; but the Master utters to one of them
the notable words: 'Thou art Peter, and upon this
rock I will build My Church; and the gates of hell
shall not prevail against it.'—a prediction of ultimate
triumph in the face of what to human wisdom must
have seemed insurmountable obstacles.   This city,
famous for the visits and works of kings, emperors,
and victorious generals, was honoured also by the
presence of Jesus of Nazareth.   This is, however, but
one of the many strange contrasts which meet us
almost at every turn as we study the history of this
land of marvels.

The terrible energy with which the Galileans defended
Jotapata in the Jewish war ought never to be forgotten.
Vespasian tried to starve them out, but could not.   The
valley about it was so deep that the sight failed on
looking down into it.

The citizens of Gadara fought at Tarichæa.   It was
taken by Vespasian, burned, and the inhabitants massacred.

Cana was perhaps Cana of Galilee, a place memorable
to the Christian, where Josephus was at one time when
summoned to Tiberias [2].

[1] Matt. xvi. 13.   [2] *Life*, XVI., XVII.

Sepphoris was the seat of one of the Five Councils which Gabinius established to govern the nation ; it was a place of strength, and had an arsenal. The Talmud mentions an 'upper' and a 'lower' town.

At Scythopolis the 15th legion wintered after Jotapata. Josephus makes it belong to the Decapolis, of which ' it was the largest city ;' but commercially it belonged to the region of the Sea of Galilee. Both the Talmud and Josephus agree in this. Scythopolis, and certain places east of the Sea of Galilee, which are usually reckoned to Peræa, the Talmud counts to Galilee. But even if we had not this authority, the fact that they lay on or near the shore of the Lake, and would therefore add very much to its life and business, is sufficient reason for mentioning them in our estimate of Galilee.

XI.

JOSEPHUS' STATEMENT AS TO THE NUMBER OF TOWNS AND INHABITANTS PROBABLY CORRECT.

WE are fully justified in saying that the country at the time now under consideration was dotted with flourishing cities and villages, and densely settled with an industrious and enterprising people. Josephus' statement that Galilee contained two hundred and four cities and villages, the smallest of which numbered above fifteen thousand inhabitants[1],—which would raise the population to upwards of three millions,—has been often quoted ; but the truth of it has been almost universally denied, or at least doubted. It ought not to be overlooked, however, that very many of those who have questioned or disputed his testimony have not always been scrupulous to quote his exact language ; for instance, Dr. Schaff, in a note to Lange on Luke[2], says, '*four* hundred and four cities and villages ; ' McClintock and Strong[3] say, ' two hundred and *forty* cities and villages ; ' Graetz[4] says, ' smallest *city* has fifteen thousand inhabitants,' which is not the language of Josephus; and Keim says, ' according to Josephus' incredible statement.' Jahn reads 'two hundred and four cities and towns, the largest of which had one hundred and fifty thousand

---

[1] *Life*, XLV. 　　　　　　　[2] Page 49, col. 1.
[3] *Cyclopædia*, vol. iii. p. 717, col. 2, art. ' Galilee.' 　　　[4] III. p. 392.

and the smallest fifteen thousand inhabitants,' as if from Josephus, but the statement is not in Josephus at all.

We propose to give several reasons, never before presented, why the statement of Josephus should be regarded as probably correct and reliable.

1. Josephus, as the military governor of Galilee, was intelligent, shrewd, and capable ; and he would be likely to know thoroughly the resources of his own province. Besides, this was at a very critical period, when the national existence was at stake, and when it was necessary that the entire strength of the country should be rallied for defence.

2. This statement of his was made in a letter which he wrote to his enemies or rivals, who had been sent from Jerusalem to supersede him in his command, who were likewise familiar with the country, and who would have detected him in any misstatement of that kind.

This fact we regard as of great weight, in reference to which we may appropriately quote Josephus' own words, used on another occasion, that—'to publish a falsehood among such as could at once detect it, would be to insure disgrace.'

3. Josephus raised without difficulty an army 'of above a hundred thousand young men.' It appears from the same passage that, in addition to these troops, there were garrisons in the various fortresses which the general had repaired and strengthened. Nineteen such places are mentioned as having been fortified by Josephus, or by his orders. Besides, he is particular to say 'young men,' showing that the supply of men was so great as to make it unnecessary, even in this extreme

national emergency, to call upon boys or old men, or others still, who were unfit for military duty. Without doing any violence to the language of Josephus, we might conclude from it that, in addition to the men under arms, there was another body equal in number to these, who were 'detained at home to provide supplies' for those in the field. Indeed, Jost, in his *Geschichte der Israeliten*, makes the number of men enrolled to be two hundred thousand, which the words of Josephus seem to justify, and which certainly cannot be disproved.

4. In the affair of the robbery of the steward of Agrippa and Berenice, when the people of the towns near Tarichæa were greatly incensed against Josephus for his part in the matter, 'one hundred thousand assembled in a single night to oppose him.'

5. When, after the conquest under Joshua, the four tribes settled in that country which afterwards became Galilee, they numbered within their limits sixty-nine cities 'with their villages.' Many of these cities were at that time fortified ; a fact elsewhere noticed.

6. By a census of that date, the tribes occupying this territory mustered 223,600 fighting men[1].

7. The slabs from Nineveh say that in the days of Hezekiah, King of Judah, Sennacherib 'took from him forty-six strong fenced cities, and of smaller towns a countless number,' besides carrying off 'more than two hundred thousand captives.'

8. In the year A.D. 39, when Herod Antipas was being tried at Rome, charged with preparing to levy war

[1] Josh xix. 10-39.

against the Romans, it was developed in the evidence
that in a single armoury he had armour collected for
seventy thousand men.   This was in a time of compara-
tive peace, and there is no contradiction of this important testimony.   What might have been its resources in
this respect when the whole province was rallying to
defend the common country?

9. If we look forward a few years, we shall find a very
significant hint. · One would suppose that the Jewish
nation in the terrible war of A.D. 66-70, so far as Palestine was concerned, had become almost entirely extinct,
the towns destroyed, and the people slaughtered.   Yet,
only sixty-three years later, an army of two hundred
thousand men rallied under the banner of Bar Cochab in
rebellion against Rome.   Julius Severus, the best general
of the empire, was sent to crush this rebellion.   He
reported to the emperor that the rebels were in
possession of fifty of the strongest castles and nine
hundred and eighty-five villages.   This struggle, which
lasted probably three years, cost the Jews upwards of
five hundred and eighty thousand lives.   The loss on
the part of the Romans was also terrible, insomuch that
Hadrian, in his despatches to the Senate announcing the
conclusion of the war, refrained from the usual congratu-
latory phrases.   If the rebels had fifty strongholds and
nine hundred and eighty-five villages in their possession
in all Judæa, then in the prosperous years before A.D. 66
Galilee may well have had two hundred and four cities
and villages [1].

[1] Milman, *History of the Jews*, II. pp. 431-438 ; Jost, *Judenthum*, II.
p. 79 ; *Dion Cassius*, lxix. 15, ' Hadrian.'

10. Captain Burton, in his *Unexplored Syria,*—a country which was full of life in Christ's time, but of which very little is known from history,—speaking of the abundance of ruins with which the region just north of Galilee is covered, says, that to one standing on a certain Lebanon peak which overlooks that section, 'the land must in many places have appeared to be one continuous town[1].'

11. Still further north, in the 'Alah, i.e. the 'high-land' of Syria, north-east and south-east of Hamah, there are three hundred and sixty-five ruined towns. The Arabs declare 'that a man might formerly have travelled for a year in this district, and never have slept twice in the same village[2].'

12. A remark similar to that of Captain Burton, just quoted, has been made in regard to the Phœnician coast, which lay west of Galilee, and with which Galilee was in such close connection, namely: 'It was so thickly covered with towns and villages that it must have given the appearance of being one unbroken city[3].'

13. If we go east of the Jordan into Peræa and the Decapolis, we find a country that in former times was more thickly dotted with cities and towns than any other portion of Syria of equal size, or any other section of the globe. In the Hauran alone, corresponding to ancient Bashan, the Arabs claim that there are one thousand of these ruined places.

14. It should also be remembered that in those times the *cities* were usually *packed* with people. In our day

---

[1] I. p. 79   [2] *Ibid.* II. p. 160.
[3] Schroder, *Die Phönizische Sprache,* 1869, Einleitung, p. 3.

we are hardly able to appreciate this fact, and certainly we do not make allowance enough for it in judging of the number of inhabitants of any given Eastern city or country as reported in the old histories. For instance, no modern city of the size of ancient Jerusalem would have held, much less accommodated, the number of people which often flocked there to attend the feasts. A few years before the siege under Titus an estimate was made, and the official return was 2,565,000 persons present at the Passover. Josephus says 2,700,000, which did not include many sick and defiled persons, and many foreigners who had come for religious worship. Some recent measurements of Dr. Thomas Chaplin, of Jerusalem, throw much light on this apparently remarkable statement of the Jewish historian.

15. Perhaps a hint may be obtained by noticing the number killed in the various battles and sieges of Galilee, so far as these were reported. We have made a careful estimate, and find the whole number to be about 155,630. This includes the prisoners, who, however, except in the case of Tarichæa, were a mere fraction. Several fights occurred where the number of killed is not given. Further, a large number of people would be destroyed in various ways in such a terrible war, and no record made of the number lost. If we put the whole number killed at one hundred and seventy-five or two hundred thousand, it cannot be regarded as an exaggeration.

In the face of such illustrative facts, the statement of Josephus in regard to the cities and villages of Galilee can no longer seem improbable.

XII.

CHARACTER OF THE GALILEANS.

1. *Thoroughly a Jewish People.*—It is by no means an easy task to describe minutely the character of this people, numbering perhaps three millions, made up as it was of many peculiar original or internal elements, and wrought upon by so many peculiar influences that were foreign or external to it. On the west were the Phœnicians, on the north the Syrians, on the south the Samaritans, and in some of the principal cities of the province were strongly marked features of Greco-Roman civilisation. Yet this remark in regard to the existence here of Greco-Roman civilisation must not be made to mean too much; for, when all the evidence on this point is collected, the real extent of such a foreign element is seen to have been very limited. The people preserved, as a body, their thoroughly Jewish character, in spite of any foreign influences tending to the contrary. It is as a Jewish people that the Galileans are to be judged. This fact is very significant. Those elements of national character by which a people is preserved from blending with those with whom it comes in contact form an interesting topic for study. Perhaps the tenacity with which the Jew held to his religious ideas might

tend to exclusiveness and bigotry.   Yet while he
would not allow interference in the affairs of his
religion, he prided himself upon his noble treatment
of strangers; and, as he allowed foreigners to settle
upon Jewish soil, so he claimed the corresponding
right, namely, to be allowed to go and settle wherever
men were.   In Christ's time one might have spoken
with truth of the omnipresent Jew. 'The Jews had
made themselves homes in every country, from the
Tiber to the Euphrates, from the pines of the Caucasus to
the spice-groves of happy Arabia[1].'   A mere catalogue
of the cities where they had settled at that time—in the
Far East, in Egypt, in Syria, in Greece and her islands—
is astonishing.   With but few exceptions, they seem to
have been everywhere a wealthy, and, in general, an
influential class.   The decrees issued from time to time
by the Roman Senate, favouring or honouring the Jews
in the different cities of the empire, were very numerous,
and throw much light upon their numbers, character,
prosperity, and their civil and social relations and standing.   A number of these are preserved by Josephus.   If
one should say that the Jews were bigoted in regard to
religion, he should remember at the same time, that, in
regard to social, commercial, and political relations, none
were more cosmopolitan in either sentiment or practice
than they.   And if the Jewish people deserve any credit
for this cosmopolitan spirit, perhaps the praise should be
given to the Galileans, who, on account of their peculiar
surroundings, must have led the way in this friendly
intercourse with other nations.   It will be important to

[1] Merivale, *Romans under the Empire*, III. p. 287.

remember this point when we come to consider the religious character of this people.

Greek influence in Palestine in Christ's time can be reduced, we think, to a very small amount. The decided contempt of the Jews, as a nation, for all foreign languages, learning, science, history, &c., would tend to preserve their Jewish character, their religion, and peculiar customs intact. They preserved their national character free from foreign influences to a far greater degree than many are disposed to admit, and made efforts in the first century after Christ to maintain among themselves a thorough knowledge of the Biblical Hebrew.

Gadara and Hippos are spoken of as Greek cities. The Syrians in Scythopolis seem to have been a majority. The 'Strangers' in Tarichæa were not necessarily foreigners, but new-comers, in distinction from old settlers. The Greeks in Tiberias were a small fraction of the whole population. In Judæa also, Gaza was a Greek city, and in Cæsarea both Syrians and Greeks were numerous. On Syrian and Phœnician cities, see *Ant.*, XIII. xv. 4. Syrians hated the Jews.

2. *Chiefly an Agricultural People.*—Further, it is chiefly as an agricultural people that we must regard them. There was, indeed, in that period, a vast amount of public building going on (under Herod the Great, Antipas, and Philip), which would require and occupy many men; secondly, we must reckon the lake commerce, which was considerable; thirdly, the fisheries (important, as we have seen); fourthly, the carrying

trade—transporting the productions of the country to foreign markets, and also merchandise between Egypt and Damascus. It is an important fact that whatever was landed from Ptolemais for Damascus, and whatever came from Egypt bound for Damascus or the Far East, and merchandise from the Far East and Damascus, bound for Egypt or Rome, would always, or at least generally, pass through Galilee. Add to these, dyeing, weaving, stone-cutting, ship-building, pottery manufacture, and a few other industries. But when we have made a sufficient deduction for all these methods of employment, we shall have left still the bulk of the population, whose business was agriculture.

An interesting topic to follow out would be the estimation in which labour was held by the people of Galilee. Cicero said of manual labour, 'there is nothing liberal in it.' A sentiment directly the opposite of this was inculcated by the teaching and practice of our Lord. The inhabitants of the northern province appear to have been an earnest, busy, and laborious class. Its wealth and prosperity, together with the good order, both civil and social, which prevailed there, would seem to indicate industry, enterprise, and intelligence on the part of its citizens. Under a people who believed in a personal and righteous God, and in their own personal accountability, all honest labour became honourable, and the valleys and hills of Galilee blossomed as a rose.

3. *Eminent for Patriotism and Courage.*—Among the prominent virtues of the Galileans we mention here their patriotism. If the influence of surrounding nations had

been so marked upon their character as is sometimes
claimed,—and it seems to us that Graetz, for example,
exaggerates this beyond reason,—it would have resulted
in weakening the ties which bound them to their country,
national institutions, and ideas ; but from the time of
Herod's first connection with this province in B.C. 47, to
the destruction of Jerusalem in A.D. 70, the Galileans
were among the noblest patriots of which the nation
could boast.   Had this patriotism been wanting in
them, even in the least degree, the fact would have
been developed greatly to their prejudice in the Jewish
war ; but in that struggle the Galileans made a noble
record.   Their intense devotion to ' the national idea '
has been spoken of as ' hot-blooded.'

Also their loyalty and devotion to their rulers, and
their bravery, for which they were justly celebrated, may
properly be considered in connection with the topic just
mentioned.   To the young governor, Herod, they were
warmly attached.   When he was appointed king, this
province declared almost unanimously in his favour.
Again, the fact that Antipas held the government forty-
three years without special complaint from his subjects,
shows a people well-disposed towards a ruler who, whatever may be said of his morals, was, *as a ruler*, liberal,
energetic, and capable in every sense.   Still later, the
devotion of the Galileans to Josephus was made by him
a matter of special praise.   Their interest in him, and
their anxiety for his welfare, outweighed all considera-
tions of peril or loss of property to themselves.   The
instances illustrating this statement are numerous.   In
praising their bravery, Josephus says that ' cowardice

was never a characteristic of the Galileans.' Aristobulus
II. and Herod the Great found here some of their most
valiant soldiers; and the deeds of the patriot army
under Josephus exhibited a marvellous contempt of
danger and death. A bold, hardy, industrious race
always does heroic deeds, when fully roused and struggling for its fatherland and freedom. This was pre-
eminently the case with the Galileans. Their character
as developed in that struggle may be taken as a hint as
to what, for perhaps many generations, had been the
character of their ancestors.

In judging the Galileans in that war, we must not
use the same standards that we judge the Romans by.
Difference of race, of civilisation, and of national purpose,
must all be considered. It was an agricultural people
matched against the finest military people of the world.
Among the Galileans the discipline was poor. They
fought, as Orientals have always done, with fiery courage,
and splendid individual valour, but with a painful lack
of system. Still, taken at this great disadvantage, they
command our highest admiration. Josephus is aware
that his force is not sufficient to cope with the Romans,
and he calls upon Jerusalem for reinforcements, but
none are sent. Galilee must alone and unaided bear
the brunt of the war during the first year of its pro-
gress. It must be remembered that this period is that
of Rome's greatest power. Yet the Emperor Nero is
'seized with consternation and alarm' at the magnitude
of the revolt. The feeling at Rome is expressed
by the fact that Vespasian, the best general of the
empire, is chosen to deal with this rebellion; and,

secondly, by the fact that such a powerful army of veterans is thought necessary to be massed at Ptolemais before operations can begin The sight of these sixty thousand veterans, among whom there is the perfection of discipline, and who are backed by the moral power of almost uninterrupted victory, must send dismay to the hearts of those Galilean youths. This splendid army that has been victorious over every nation, and whose engines have levelled the foremost structures in the world, has come hither to try its strength and skill upon the people and fortresses of Galilee The abandonment with which the Galileans plunge into this struggle admits of no retreat. To restore their country's ancient liberty is the wild dream of those brave, misguided men. The tough work before them seems to serve as a stimulus to greater boldness. At Jotapata they fight with desperate energy The one hundred and sixty projectile engines of the Romans fill the air with murderous stones and other implements of death. Even after forty days of almost superhuman valour, but which is seen to be unavailing, these patriots still prefer 'to die for liberty' and 'their country's glory' rather than surrender. For six terrible hours the 'fighting men' of Japha—the largest 'village' of Galilee—beat back the Roman soldiers, till 'twelve thousand' of the former were consumed. The struggle at Gamala is one of the most heroic of the war. Tiberias, Tarichæa, Mount Tabor, Gischala, fall in succession The fate of Jotapata, it was said, sealed the fate of the whole of Judæa The backbone of the rebellion was broken when Galilee was subdued. The hardest fighting of the war was done by these brave people of the north. That for her may well be called a bloody year, in which one hundred and fifty thousand or more of her people perished. The flower of her youth had fallen. The conduct of the Galileans calls forth generous criticisms even from their victorious enemies. Vespasian notices their fidelity to each other and their contempt of suffering, and Titus admits 'that they are fighting for freedom and country,' and that 'they bear up bravely in disaster.' He even appeals to their example as a means of stimulating his own veteran troops. The Romans had reason to be proud of the conquest of Galilee. But their army was weary, and its ranks thinned from the bloody work of this campaign, and Vespasian was obliged to order time for rest and recruiting.

A very minute and vivid account of the organisation and discipline of the Roman army is given by Josephus. Of the size of the army, Tacitus gives the forces of the Romans as follows: 5th, 10th, 15th, and 3rd, 12th, 22nd legions; 20 cohorts of allies; 8 squadrons of horse; also two kings, Agrippa and Sohemus; Antiochus sent the forces of his kingdom; also 'a formidable body of Arabs with embittered feelings' took part; and a 'considerable number of volunteers went from Rome and Italy.' Graetz makes the army about Jerusalem number 80,000 men. Weber and Holtzmann quote Hausrath's brilliant description of the character of the two armies and the contrast between them, and also Gfrörer's, from his Preface to the *Jewish War* of Josephus.

4. *Their Ancestors Eminent for Bravery.*—The bravery of which we have seen such wonderful exhibitions seems to have been a characteristic of the people of this region from remote times. Their position made them the first to suffer in case of those great invasions from the East, a circumstance which would naturally have a tendency to foster bravery in them. 'Zebulun and Naphtali were a people that jeoparded their lives unto the death in the high places of the field[1].' Within the limits of this province were embraced some of the most memorable battle-fields of the nation. A people among whom national and traditional customs were cherished as dearer than life would not be indifferent to old memories and historical associations ; and hence the Galileans could not but be stimulated by the noble deeds that had been wrought by their ancestors upon their own soil. The Plain of Jezreel was a famous field of strife. Kishon was a river of battle. Deborah and Barak led down from Tabor ten thousand heroes against the King of Hazor, and routed his general, Sisera, and his army. Zebulun, Naphtali, and Asher followed Gideon in the storm against Midian. Soon after the division of the kingdom of Solomon, the princes of Zebulun and Naphtali, in common with those of Benjamin and Judah, led their heroes against Moab. And in the final struggle with Rome, these bold and independent sons of the north rallied, as we have seen, first and foremost to oppose the invincible legions, and battled with desperate energy from mountain-pass to mountain-pass, from city to city, from fortress to

[1] Judges v. 18.

fortress, till one after another the cities and fortresses
of this province were beaten into ruins; and then, as
the nation rallied for a death-grapple with the enemy,
the remnants of the Galilean band joined their countrymen behind the walls of Jerusalem, and resisted with
superhuman might that all-conquering power, as it
slowly, but surely, beat down the walls, and even
overturned 'the foundations of Zion,' burying city
and Temple and their heroic defenders in a common
ruin.

5. *Their Great Respect for Law and Order.*—Again,
the Galileans are to be thought of as peaceable and
law-abiding citizens. The impression is sometimes
given that the very opposite of this was the case.
Thus Ritter speaks of the people of Tiberias 'as
always in quarrels with the parent city of Jerusalem,'
for which no authority is given, and which is contrary
to fact. And Hausrath, usually correct, states that
Josephus calls the Galileans 'common peace-disturbers
of the land,' whereas Josephus is referring directly to
the robbers in certain caves, which Herod had subdued.
Because Galilee was the home of Judas the Zealot,
Graetz states that 'the land was full of hot-heads,'
thus giving a very wrong impression. Of these, the
second reference is wrong; the first is an isolated case
that happened in Jerusalem, and does not by any
means represent the character of the Galileans; in the
last Josephus simply says, 'trained to war from their
infancy,'—meaning that the Galileans, although chiefly
an agricultural people, were obliged, on account of the
people about them, to be acquainted to some extent

with military affairs. Josephus does not state, nor say anything from which we might infer, that the Galileans were 'turbulent' and 'rebellious,' or that they delighted in 'warfare'; he says nothing of the kind , and the impression left after several careful readings of Josephus is as we have stated—that they were peaceable and law-abiding citizens.   Indeed, Josephus makes a careful distinction between the inhabitants on the border and the robbers, and shows that the former were not in sympathy with the latter, but were greatly harassed by them.   After Herod had crushed them, 'Galilee was delivered from its apprehensions;' which statement confirms what we have said.   The Syrians even (Galilee's neighbours on the north) sung songs in honour of Herod on this occasion, showing that they, as well as the Galileans, were not in sympathy with the robbers.   Those robber bands on the border, secreted in caves—'dens of thieves'—the guerillas of that age, —we hear almost nothing of after Herod made such thorough work in subduing them.

Again, about the year A D. 51, certain commotions arose in various parts of the land, to which Josephus alludes ; and in the same connection he speaks of one occasion when the Galileans, on their way to a feast at Jerusalem, were assaulted near Ginæa by some Samaritans, and one or more of the former were killed.   On account of the negligence of Cumanus, the Roman governor, very serious trouble grew out of this affair. But the affair itself has been greatly exaggerated.   For instance Keim says: 'The Galileans were often obliged to open by force a way through the Samaritan district, when they would go to the feasts at Jerusalem[1].' And Hausrath likewise gives the impression that such events were of frequent occurrence. But this event appears to have been an isolated instance ; at least, there is no evidence to the contrary, while considerable evidence could be produced to show some intercourse and many friendly acts between the Galileans and the Jews of Judæa on one side, and the Samaritans on the other.' Furthermore, it is wholly wrong to say that 'the Sicarii committed more crimes in Galilee than in Judæa[2].' The very opposite was true.

Perhaps the following summary will set the real state of affairs before the reader's mind.

During the long reign of Herod the Great, Galilee enjoyed prosperity and quiet. The same was true of it, with perhaps one exception—Antipas' war with Aretas —during the longer reign of Herod Antipas. During this latter period, the country east of the Jordan, which was ruled by the mild and honourable Herod Philip, also enjoyed peace and prosperity. But Judæa, from the death of Herod the Great, in B.C. 4, to the outbreak of the war in A.D. 66, was full of commotion. The great contrast between affairs in the north and in the south is strikingly apparent in Josephus' account of these times, although the contrast itself is never alluded to by him. From A.D. 7 to the time of the war, Judæa was ruled by Roman governors (except the short period covered by the reign of Agrippa I., A.D. 41 to 44), who, for the most part, were unprincipled and cruel men. They hated, oppressed, insulted, and wronged the Jews in many ways.

[1] I. p. 313.   [2] Neubauer, p. 183.

They countenanced robbery, whenever they could receive a share of the plunder. They encouraged the system of bribery. Under them the priests became corrupt. Murder, violence, lawlessness of all kinds prevailed more and more. The conduct of these governors was very exasperating to the Jews; and at last, however little disposed for war they were at first, they were driven to take up arms, considering an honourable death better than a miserable life. But such long-continued misrule could hardly fail of generating misery and corruption. And in our estimate of Galilee it is never to be forgotten that, while up to A D. 51, or perhaps 55, this province was in a state of peace and prosperity, the province of Judæa, on the other hand, had, for half a century, lacked both law and order, and there had come to prevail a terrible state of licence and anarchy.

The Jews are oppressed by the Romans, and wronged by Felix, who takes Drusilla from her husband for his own wife. Lawlessness and corruption increase, and the Jews are driven to madness. The country suffers much in many ways, and robbers are encouraged. Judæa is overrun by robbers, and every section of the country is infested by them. The Romans hate the Jews, and insult them. Florus' conduct is violent and exasperating, and the same is true of Sabinius', of Patronius', and of Pilate's. The great financial crisis in Rome in A.D. 33 affects Palestine. The priests become corrupt, and the poorer priests are left to suffer and die. By the violence of Florus, the Jews are forced to leave the country; yet Cumanus does the Jews a favour. But in this case he could hardly have refused to interfere. Vitellius also does them favours. The Sikars, who were assassins with concealed weapons, *sica*, hence *Sicarii*, originated in Jerusalem.

The revolt of Judas, son of Hezekias, on the death of Herod the Great, has sometimes been referred to as showing the turbulent spirit of the Galileans. But the commotions at the time were widespread, and by no means confined to one section ; Judas in Galilee gets possession of Sepphoris ; Simon makes an insurrection in Peræa, crosses the Jordan, and burns the palace in Jericho ; two thousand of Herod's old soldiers make an insurrection in Idumæa ; Athronges in Judæa sets himself up as king ; four parties in four different sections of the country keep the nation in tumult ; all these are in addition to the fierce outbreak at the Feast of Pentecost that year, May 31, B.C. 4.

F

XIII.

RELIGION, EDUCATION, AND MORALS AMONG THE GALILEANS

WE come now to speak of the religious character of the Galileans, with which may be associated the kindred topics of morals and education. On these points we would not presume to speak, except after the most careful study. It is a most difficult matter to separate the Galileans from the people of Judæa, and say that they possessed this or that characteristic, in distinction from the latter. Still, there is evidence to enable us to do this to some extent; at least, it can be shown that the Galileans were equally interested with the Judæans in all matters pertaining to education and religion. Indeed, in some respects, the advantage in regard to religion and morals will be found to be on the side of the Galileans. The impression is often given that away from the Temple, in the far northern province, ignorance and irreligion prevailed. The statement is made that 'they manifested less aversion to the religion and manners of the heathen than the people of the south, and less zeal for the religion of Moses[1].' Also, that 'from their heathen neighbours the Galileans imbibed all sorts of superstitions. Nowhere else were

---

[1] Munk, p. 33, col. 1.

there so many persons possessed and plagued with evil spirits as in Galilee ; since the Galilean narrow-mindedness ascribed all forms of disease to the influence of demons [1].' Their religious character is further described as a singular mixture of faith and superstition. It is supposed that before the destruction of Jerusalem this province was especially poor in regard to means for disseminating knowledge (understand, *knowledge of the law of Moses*, the only thing which 'knowledge' meant to the Jews), and on this account 'the Galileans were stricter and more tenacious in regard to customs and morals' than the people of the south. Neubauer tells us that, on account of the picturesque scenery and delightful climate of Galilee, the mind, away from the influence of the religious formalism which existed in Jerusalem, would naturally devote itself. more to parables and legends. This writer goes so far as to state that 'this province possessed no wise men, still less a school,' for which, however, he gives no authority.

We are not prepared to accept these statements, nor any one of them, as final in this matter. The first two, those of Graetz and Munk, are decidedly wrong. But since, among the Jews, 'education' meant merely *education in religion*, the two naturally blend together in our treatment of them. That passage in Josephus is very significant which states that during the reign of Queen Alexandra (B.C. 79–70, or 78-69) the Pharisees rose to power—'a sect reputed to excel all others in the accurate explanation of the laws.' This means no less

----

[1] Graetz, III. p. 395.

than that there was, at that time, a revival of Biblical
study. At the death of Herod the Great we hear of two
celebrated teachers, Judas and Matthias, whose 'explanation of the laws many young men attended.' But they
do not appear to have taught in any special school, nor
to have belonged to any organised school system whatever. The famous Hillel was not trained for a teacher ;
but he began to teach, and the result proved his natural
fitness for that work. Neither Hillel nor Gamaliel, the
teacher of young Saul, belonged to any college, seminary,
or other institution of learning, i. e. in our meaning of
those words. There could not be a school system where
instructors (here the Rabbis) were not allowed to receive
pay for their labour. Whoever understood the law
thoroughly, and had facility in explaining it, provided
he chose to teach, was regarded as 'a learned man'—a
Rabbi. With regard to schools and public instruction
among the Jews, the Talmud is inclined, we think, to
ascribe too great antiquity to the Rabbinical school
system, which was developed and existed only long
after the destruction of Jerusalem, and to give the
impression that the systematic public instruction and
training of youth prevailed long before the beginning
of our era. Dr. Ginsburg[1] gives too much weight to
these statements of the Talmud, and thus misrepresents,
unintentionally no doubt, the real state of the case at the
time of Christ. In Christ's time there were no schools
which it was necessary to have attended, or at which
it was necessary to have graduated, in order to be regarded as a learned man. The only schools were those

[1] In art. 'Education,' in Kitto's *Cyclopædia Bib. Lit.*, I. p. 729.

connected with the synagogues. The only school-book was the Hebrew Scriptures. A synagogue presupposed a school, just as in our country a church presupposes a Sunday-school. Church and district-school is not a parallel to the Jewish system of things, but church and Sunday-school is. Synagogues were found in every city throughout the land, and also in every village, unless the place was insignificant in size; and even in such cases they had their place or places of prayer. At one time Tiberias boasted of thirteen synagogues, and Jerusalem of four hundred and eighty.

The method in the schools, so far as there was any, was nearly as follows: Questions were asked and answered, opinions stated and discussed, and illustrations proposed in the form of allegories, aphorisms, or parables; corresponding, perhaps, as much as anything modern, to our adult Bible-classes[1]. In the training of boys much responsibility and labour devolved upon the father. The boy was afterwards sent to these Bible-class meetings, which constituted the schools of the land, and which existed wherever there was a synagogue. Philo says: 'What else are the synagogues than schools of piety and virtue?' Hausrath calls them 'the true schools of the nation.' Jerusalem, as the metropolis of the nation, would no doubt exert, in many respects, a dominant influence. The most eminent teachers would naturally go there, as in the case of Hillel and Gamaliel. But Sepphoris and Tiberias, the capitals in succession of Galilee, would have their eminent teachers as well; whilst every town and village

[1] Luke ii. 46; xx. 2-4; see Matt. xxii. 17-22.

might boast of its learned men—its local Rabbis or
Rabbi. How often it is said that Christ went through
all the cities and villages of Galilee, teaching in the
schools or synagogues, and preaching the gospel of the
kingdom[1]! Again, on a certain occasion in Capernaum,
'there were Pharisees and doctors of the law sitting by,
who were come out of every town (κώμη) of Galilee and
Judæa and Jerusalem[2].' Sometimes the learned men of
the south and the north would visit each other for friendly
intercourse, when, according to Keim, they were treated
with respect by the people, and given the places of
honour in the synagogues. The Scribes of the south
would also visit the north to watch Christ; not to see if
the law was fulfilled, but to see if their traditions were
violated[3].

The Talmud charges the Galileans with neglecting
tradition[4], and the passages in the Gospels just referred
to show that there was some ground for such a charge
in Christ's time. Further, this charge and the visits of
the Jerusalem doctors just referred to, both show that
while Jerusalem, where were the Temple and the Sanhedrin, exercised a dominant influence in reference to
matters of religion, yet the Galileans were in a measure
independent of it in this respect. A just distinction
to make is this : that in Jerusalem were the champions
of tradition, and in Galilee the champions of the law.
Adherence to the strict letter of the law may be regarded
as a prominent characteristic of the learned men of
Galilee, in distinction from those of Jerusalem[5]. In

---

[1] Matt. ix. 35, and many other places.   [2] Luke v. 17.
[3] Matt. xvi. ; Mark vii. 1.   [4] Neubauer, p. 183.   [5] Matt. v. 17, 18

Jerusalem novelties were introduced and changes made, according to emergencies, and sometimes licenses allowed, in regard to religious and other usages, which would not be tolerated in Galilee.

If we may refer to Christ in this connection, perhaps the remarks just made will be illustrated by His wonderful familiarity with the Scriptures, His great regard for the law, and His contempt for tradition. The Scribes and learned men of Galilee, so far as we can judge, were familiar with the law; worship in the synagogues was strictly maintained ; and there appears to have existed here a freer and healthier and religious life than in the south. Among the different sects in Jerusalem Christ met with an atmosphere that was cheerless and dismal. In the freer north, far away from the bleak home of priests and Levites, there was a people less ·under the influence of the 'straiter' sects, less hardened and narrowed by the dogmatic systems which prevailed in the holy city ; among which people Christ for the most part found a welcome. Without seeking to draw too sharp a distinction between the people of Galilee and those of Judæa, it is no doubt true that the former lacked the narrow prejudices of the latter towards the people of other nations ; for, to mention a single instance, it is a worthy son of the north who, at Joppa, in a wonderful vision, first learns and teaches to his countrymen that great lesson of the Master, that the Gentiles, as well as themselves, may share in the new gospel of the grace of God[1]. And, in general, the influences in Galilee tended to develop and enlarge the national mind and character,

[1] Acts x.

while those in Judæa tended to contract and dwarf
the same. The peasants and shepherds on the rather
poor uplands of Judæa are spoken of as ignorant and
narrow—the slavish tools of the priesthood of Jerusalem
—the fuel easily kindled into ' uproars of the people[1].'
In Josephus, *Wars*, IV. iii. 8, a case is mentioned where
brigands ' drag a rustic from the country,' who ' scarcely
knew what the high-priesthood meant,' for the purpose
of making him high-priest.

In regard to the violation of the laws pertaining to
marriage, public sentiment seems to have been a unit
throughout the land. The case of Antipas and John the
Baptist furnishes an illustration. The custom of the
Jews was a peculiar one: a man who did not marry a
deceased brother's widow in case there had been no
children, was a criminal; but such marriage, in case there
had been children, was itself criminal! Again, a man
might divorce his wife; but if a wife divorced her husband
it was a public abomination ! Herodias divorced herself
from Herod Philip (*not* the tetrarch), ' confounding the
laws of our country.' Archelaus also scandalised the
nation by marrying his brother's widow, *when she had
children by her first husband.* Also, that morbid sensi-
tiveness of the Jews in regard to images and statues was
shared in by the people of the whole country alike. The
people of Tiberias, when Caius wanted his statue put
up in the Temple, ' stretched out their throats, and
were ready to die;' 'they left off tilling the ground;'
and 'the land remained unsown.' Several particulars,
however, are mentioned in regard to morals and certain

[1] Matt. xxvi. 5.

other things which show a greater degree of strictness in Galilee than in Judæa. For instance, the great care of the Galileans was for reputation, while the Judæans cared less for reputation, and more for money. We regard this statement as all the more significant, because it was made by the ancient Rabbis themselves. Also, as to labouring on Passover eves, some synagogical rites, devoting goods directly to God, and not to the priests, funeral customs, provision for widows, marriages being celebrated with decorum, a spirit of charity or benevolence, and as to regulations in regard to the intercourse of betrothed persons—in all these respects, greater strictness is conceded to the Galileans.

That the Galileans 'manifested less zeal for the religion of Moses' than the people of the south, we have shown to be incorrect. Rather the contrary was true. The statement that they imbibed all sorts of superstitions from their heathen neighbours, as 'possession of devils' and the like, has not the slightest evidence in its support, either in Josephus or the New Testament. The statement stands as an assertion without proof. As to 'means for disseminating a knowledge of the law,' Galilee was as well provided as Judæa ; aside, perhaps, from certain eminent teachers in Jerusalem, with whom, however, it is not possible that all the learned men of Christ's time could have studied. Still, it is said that they were less 'sensitive to heathen influences,' and that a 'heathen city like Tiberias would not have been tolerated in Judæa.' The facts will not justify these assertions. There were theatres and amphitheatres in many of the large cities of the country. In the splendid theatre and the vast amphitheatre at Jerusalem were enacted all the games that were known in Italy or Greece, while Tiberias, so far as we know, had only a stadium, or racecourse. If by being 'less sensitive to heathen influences' is meant that, apart from religious ideas, the commercial and social ideas of the Galileans were broadened and benefited by their intercourse with surrounding nations, then the statement is true. Such a result was produced by that intercourse.

As to the influence of the morals of the rulers on those of the people, there are but few data from which to judge. Alexandra, Hyrcanus' daughter, seems to have been destitute of principle in her attempt to administer by her beautiful children, Aristobulus and Mariamne, to the lust of Antony, of whom she wanted some favour. As to Herod the Great, whatever else may have been his crimes, he could never be charged with either lust or intemperance. Herod Philip was a man of whose morals no ill could be said. Archelaus' reign was short. Under the Romans, from A D 7 to 66, Judæa, as we have seen, suffered in every way. Herod Antipas was neither lustful nor intemperate. His act in marrying Herodias (a violation of the law, because she had a child by her first husband, Antipas' brother) was universally condemned, and by no means imitated by his subjects. To the credit of both Herodias and Antipas, it should be said that they loved each other truly, and when Antipas was banished, and Herodias might have lived in ease in Rome or Judæa, she chose to follow her husband into exile—an act which, if people were not prejudiced against her, would be spoken of as noble.

In addition to what has been said, we are to consider:
1. That Christ was, as a rule, well received in Galilee;
2. That John the Baptist had here a strong party of
adherents; 3. That this was the home of Judas, the
founder of the sect of the Galileans. Although he
founded his sect in Jerusalem, he is mentioned in the
New Testament only in Acts v. 37; his rallying theme
was, that God alone was Master; paying tribute to the
Romans was slavery; they were 'not to bow to mortals
as their masters.' Graetz [1] says of this Judas that 'in
consequence of his life and deeds the masters of the
world had so much more trouble to subdue the small
Jewish people than they did to subdue the great nations
of Europe.' This man's moral character cannot be
impugned; he was a Puritan of the strictest school; the
platform of his sect or party looked well on paper,—a
grand idea about which to rally, but it was thoroughly
impracticable in those unfortunate times; 4. That this
was the home, also, of Eleazar, the missionary to Adiabene and the court of Izates. This man 'was very
skilful in the learning of his country.' His words, 'not
only to read the law, but to practise it,' represent the
thorough style of his teaching. He seems to have been
zealous, familiar with the law, skilful and eloquent in
presenting his views; and perhaps we have a right to
regard him as a representative man of Galilee.

Again, we hold the opinion that the Sermon on the
Mount, whether regarded as one discourse, or as the
substance of many discourses, could not have been
preached in Judæa—at the beginning of Christ's

[1] *Sinai et Golgotha*, Paris, 1867, p. 267.

ministry, at least—considering the fact that Jerusalem
was the hot-bed of tradition, and considering, also, the
excited state of the public mind there, wild as it was
with dreams of the coming Messiah. The sermon presupposes the ability, and also a willingness, on the part
of the listeners, to look beyond tradition and the mere
letter of the law, to a somewhat new and enlarged appli-
cation of old sayings and truths. Such a state of mind
would not be looked for in Judæa at that time ; but we
should expect just that in the region of Capernaum.

On the general character of the people of Judæa as
distinguished from those of Galilee, and how easily they
were misled by false Messiahs—strange proceedings such
as were never reported from Galilee—see passage in
Hausrath [1]. It would have been difficult for Christ to
have planted Himself in Judæa.

[1] *Neutestamentliche Zeitgeschichte*, I. pp 41, 42

XIV.

THE POETICAL TALENT FINELY DEVELOPED AMONG THE GALILEANS.

BESIDES the physical and moral vigour of this people, we discover, also, an elasticity and freshness of spirit which did not prevail among the people of the south. On this account it was, perhaps, that here the poetical talent was so finely developed. We have already quoted the statement that, 'if Nature could influence mind, if it could create genius, Naphtali would be a land of poets.' 'The vine-covered slopes, the plains brilliant with flowers, the wooded glens and knolls, sparkling with springs,' the beautiful lake deep within the bosom of the hills, the distant but ever visible 'great sea'—symbol of the Infinite—would all contribute to awaken and stimulate the richest, and perhaps grandest, spirit of poetry. One of the earliest triumph-songs of Israel, as well as one of the noblest, sounded forth from the hills of Galilee on the occasion of Barak's victory over the Canaanites in the Plain of Jezreel. And, if we were to adopt the view held by many eminent scholars (Gesenius and others), the Song of Songs had also its origin among these beautiful scenes of Nature—the music of a heart about which earth and sky had lavished their charms—the song of one whose eyes delighted in beholding the beauty of the flowers, and the richness of the fig-tree, the olive, and the vine.

XV.

THE PROPHETS, JUDGES, AND OTHER FAMOUS MEN OF GALILEE.

IN this connection a brief notice must be taken of the famous persons whose birthplace, or home, was in this northern province. We may be obliged here to go beyond the strict limits of our period, in order to answer the flippant and prejudiced remark: 'Out of Galilee ariseth no prophet[1]'—a remark which should never have been believed at all, but which, being accepted without reflection, has had much influence in shaping the common notion of the character of Galilee. In the time of the Judges, Naphtali furnished Barak, the victor over the Canaanites, with whom should be mentioned Deborah, 'a prophetess,' the 'mother in Israel' whose presence and words inspired those bold sons of the north to heroic deeds, and also Jael, 'the wife of Heber the Kenite,' a heroine of that bloody day[2]. Zebulun furnished Ibzan, who judged Israel seven years, and after him Elon, who judged Israel for ten years. Issachar likewise furnished Tola, who judged Israel twenty-three years[3]. Still later this country sent forth a number of prophets, whose memories were always cherished by the people, and whose tombs were built and guarded by a grateful

---

[1] John vii. 52.　　[2] Judges iv.　　[3] Judges x. 1, 2; xii. 8, 11.

posterity with pious care. If it is doubtful whether
Elijah was born in Galilee, yet the scene of his labours
was chiefly this northern region, and the home of his
successor Elisha was in the tribe of Issachar. Hosea
also belonged to Issachar ; Jonah, the son of Amittai,
came from Gath Hepher in Zebulun ; and the prophet
Nahum from Elkosh in Galilee. This has been disputed ;
still many able scholars hold the view here expressed [1].
In the Assyrian captivity, under Shalmaneser, appears
Tobit from Naphtali. He was 'a godly man,' and ' in
the account of him we have a very instructive picture
both of his home and of his times.' Alexander, the
first renowned Jewish philosopher in Alexandria,—a
peripatetic and the forerunner of Philo,—is supposed
by some to have been born in Paneas. This, however,
is not certainly established.   Nitai, B.C. 140–110, a
learned doctor of the Mishna, came from Arbela.
His rule of life was : ' Avoid a bad neighbour ;
associate not with sinners ; and do not forget a future
recompense.'   Two other Mishna doctors also came
from this region, and King Alexander Jannæus, son
of Hyrcanus, calls Galilee his fatherland.

   In Christ's time, Anna the prophetess belonged to
Asher, and, we may mention again, the missionary
Eleazar and Judas the Galilean zealot, and with the
latter his sons, James and Simon, who were crucified,
and Manahem, who was killed in Jerusalem. Perhaps
Hezekiah, the brigand chief whom Herod slew, and
his son Judas, who on Herod's death raised a revolt,
took Sepphoris, and was captured only after a hard

   [1] Smith's *Bible Dict.*, I. p. 724, art. ' Elkosh.'

struggle, may be mentioned as showing, though outlaws, the mettle of the Galileans. There was also Eleazar, the son of Jairus, a kinsman of Manahem and a descendant of Judas the zealot, who was the founder of the sect of the Galileans. This Eleazar boasted of himself and his companions : 'We were the first of all to revolt,' against the Romans, 'and we are the last in arms against them' ; 'We determined to serve as master no one but God, and the time has come for us to show the sincerity of our words by our actions' ; and they all perished then and there, in the bloody slaughter at Masada. Galilee had Herod the Great for governor, afterwards Antipas, the ablest of his sons, and still later, as military governor, Josephus. At that time flourished the famous John of Gischala ; Silas, the governor of Tiberias by Josephus' appointment, and Joshua, in authority there, but opposed to Josephus ; Julius Capellus, leader of the most respectable party in Tiberias, and his associates, namely, Herod son of Miarus, Herod son of Gamalus, Compsus and Crispus—these two the sons of Compsus ; also, Pistus and his son Justus—the latter a friend of Greek learning, and the author of a history in Greek of his own times, but the implacable enemy of Josephus.

There was in the early Church a tradition that the parents of the Apostle Paul came from Gischala in Galilee. It is easy to reject the tradition, but quite difficult to see how such a tradition should become attached to this particular place ; somebody at some time must have believed it, and perhaps with reasons. We might, perhaps, include Nathanael of Cana of

Galilee ; Peter, as a representative man of Galilee ;
Zebedee and his two sons, James and John—a family
of wealth ; Andrew and Philip, of Bethsaida in Galilee ;
Joseph and Mary ; James, the brother of Christ and the
first Bishop of Jerusalem ; also Salome, sister of Mary
and wife of Zebedee.

And, if we were to look beyond the destruction of
Jerusalem, we should find Galilee the abode of many
famous and learned men, and the seat of flourishing
schools. From the second to the sixth century it was
the centre of Jewish learning in Palestine.

XVI.

THE WEALTH AND MATERIAL PROSPERITY OF THE PROVINCE.

OF the wealth and material prosperity of Galilee it is difficult to speak, apart from the connection of this topic with the whole country. Of the wealth and prosperity of the whole country during the period covered by the reign of Herod the Great and the life of Christ, very much might be said. The Jews throughout the world were a wealthy class. In wealth, as well as in numbers, they surpassed the Greeks in Cæsarea. Those in Parthia, on the Euphrates, were rich. Strabo, as quoted by Josephus, remarks upon their wealth and prosperity 'in every city in the habitable earth.' In Crete, Melos, and Rome their wealth is spoken of. Vast sums from all parts of the world flowed into the Temple at Jerusalem. In B.C. 54, Crassus took from the Temple upwards of ten thousand talents in gold and silver, and one huge ingot of gold besides. In several other instances, the Temple was robbed by the grasping Roman governors or generals. Herod the Great was one of the best financiers the world has ever seen. He was always ready with money or provisions, in case any one was in need. He was a capital provider for his own family and kingdom. Measuring his revenue by his expenses, his kingdom must have been managed with great ability to have yielded so much. He was never in debt, always remarkably prompt in his payments, frequently assisting others who were in need of money ; and from the outset of his governorship of Galilee, at the age of twenty-five, to his death, he was constantly making valuable presents to various cities or persons. It may be added that the bier, bed, and other furnishings at Herod's funeral indicate great wealth. The wealth of King Agrippa I. is also referred to. Men from other parts of the world even went to Judæa for adventure and speculation. Rich articles of gold and silver, and costly carpets and vestments, were sometimes bought in Rome for Judæa. The Romans in general had exaggerated ideas of the wealth of this country ; it was to them a sort of gold mine ; just the place where greedy Roman politicians might accumulate money or repair their fortunes.

But we must of course confine our attention to Galilee. Its material prosperity has been hinted at in our notice of the industries of the province. Its numerous and flourishing cities and villages—some of which were elegantly built—indicate the very opposite of poverty and limited means. The 'opulent' citizens of Gischala are spoken of. John of Gischala was a man of wealth, and usually shrewd and capable in business. The people of Sepphoris are described as possessed of 'ample means.' The tithes collected in Galilee are mentioned as amounting to 'a large sum of money.' The treasure stored in the palace of Antipas at Tiberias was a large amount, and the furnish-

ings of the palace were astonishingly rich and elegant.
Several times Galilee had to support a portion of the
Roman army in winter quarters : for instance, under
Silo, under Vespasian in Scythopolis, and in other cases.
The Talmud mentions three cities of Galilee which
had 'sent enormous treasures to Jerusalem—Sichin,
Caboul, and Magdala.' Zebedee, it is supposed, was
a man of wealth and influence. Capernaum, as a centre
of news, business, and commerce, was a place of luxury.
It is a significant fact that Christ chose this very
centre as His residence. The fact that Christ was called
a 'gluttonous man and a wine-bibber' shows that a
style of living prevailed here which was distasteful to
certain ascetics of the time[1]; the words in Luke
vii. 34, are φάγος καὶ οἰνοπότης. Perhaps, in Christ's
reproach of Bethsaida, Chorazin, and Capernaum, there
may be a hint as to the wealth and luxury and con-
sequent worldliness of these places. Along their 'way
of the sea' the rich fabrics, spices, and other products of Babylon and farther Asia would be carried, on
their way to Egypt or Rome, by rich merchants seeking goodly pearls[2]. Galilee would be benefited by
the traffic carried on at the trading stations along this
route of commerce.

The contribution sent from Antioch, in A.D. 44, was
from the brethren in Judæa, or perhaps for 'the poor
saints in Jerusalem,' as if no assistance was needed by
the brethren in Galilee[3]. In B.C. 43, four years after
Herod was appointed governor of Galilee, Cassius came

[1] Matt. xi. 19.   [2] Matt. xiii. 45, 46.
[3] Acts xi. 29; Rom. xv. 26.

into Syria for the purpose of raising men and money. For the latter object there was, in his view, no richer field than Judæa. The enormous sum which Crassus (B.C. 54) had taken from the Temple at Jerusalem convinced him of that. He imposed a tribute on Judæa (i. e. the whole province, including Judæa, Samaria, and Galilee) of seven hundred talents. Antipater (father of Herod the Great) distributed this among several persons, that it might be raised with all possible despatch[1]. Herod, as governor of Galilee, was the first to bring in his share, which was one hundred talents, and thus he gained the favour of Cassius, who bestowed upon him the governorship of Cœle-Syria.

When this essay was first prepared we added here the following paragraph, which, upon reconsideration, we have decided to retain. We made the suggestion only after we had examined every passage in the *Wars* and in the last seven books of the *Antiquities*, where contributions, tributes, taxes, fines, &c., are mentioned, and the amounts given. After this laborious comparison we feel justified in saying that the amount named in Josephus, 700 talents, seems small, measured by other sums which were raised at other times, and by the great distress caused by forcing the collection of this tribute. Cassius stood in pressing need of money. He had wild ideas of the wealth of the country. Certain sections were slow in making their payments, and four cities were reduced to slavery, which alone, on any reasonable computation, would have yielded a sum equal to, or greater than, the whole amount required. The cities

[1] *Wars*, I. xi. 2.

reduced to slavery were Lydda, Thamna, Gophna, and Emmaus. As an illustrative fact we may mention that Herod, after being made king, subdued the robbers in Galilee, and upon the few places which they occupied levied a tribute of 100 talents for their good behaviour. The amount taken by Crassus from the Temple alone would be at least fifteen or sixteen times greater than the tribute in question, and in the latter case it was to be collected from the whole country. We conclude that Cassius was not so urgent for money as is represented, and consequently his levy was small, or else, which seems plausible, that the text should read 7000 instead of 700, as at present. On the other hand, 7000 talents is a large amount, and would astonish us, did we not know that despots and rapacious governors place no limits to their unrighteous demands.

As to mines in Judæa, as distinguished from Galilee and Samaria, there were none. The 'iron mountain' of Josephus was east of the Jordan. Extensive copper mines, and also gold deposits, are found in the Sinaitic peninsula. Traces of a mine have been found on the south border of the Plain of Esdraelon, which would be on the border of Galilee. The north part of Galilee, at least the Lebanon region, was rich in mines, especially in iron. Deposits of lead and copper exist in the hills between the Phœnician coast and Upper Galilee. The copper mines of Cyprus were extensive, and Herod had half the revenue from them, and the care of the other half. On this topic the following references may be of value: Josephus, *Wars*, IV. viii. 2; *Ant.*, XVI. iv. 5; Ewald, *Hist. Israel*, IV. p. 192, and references to the Old

Testament ; Lightfoot, I. p. 189 ; Ritter, *Geography of Palestine*, II. p. 189 ; Smith's *Bible Dict.*, III. p. 1911, col. 1, art. 'Metals,' respecting mines in the Lebanon region ; *ibid.*, p. 1937, art. 'Mines'; Burton's *Unexplored Syria*, I. p. 31 ; II. p. 27 ; Arnaud, *La Palestine*, p. 368, *et seq.*; Burton's *Gold Mines and Ruined Cities of Midian*, London, 1878.

XVII.

WAS GALILEE REGARDED WITH CONTEMPT BY THE PEOPLE OF JERUSALEM, AS IS SO OFTEN ALLEGED?

THERE is a very general impression that the Jews of Jerusalem regarded with contempt the people of Galilee, and even the province itself. And of this scorn Nazareth received perhaps the largest share. Supposing such a feeling to have existed, all that we have hitherto said is a protest against the justice of it. In its climate, its fertile soil, and its charming scenery; in the abundance of its waters, and the beauty of its lakes; in its numerous and often elegant cities and villages; in its hardy, industrious, and intelligent population; in the interest of its people in the law, in the Temple and its services, in the great national feasts and in the general welfare of the nation; in its wealth and material prosperity, its various thriving industries, and in the unexampled patriotism and bravery of its sons,—what ground is there why the people of Jerusalem should regard Galilee or the Galileans with contempt?

But, in order to show how universally it has been taken for granted that this feeling existed, it is necessary to quote a few statements both from scholars and from popular writers as well. We include such as refer to both Nazareth and Galilee: 'Peter was a Galilean fisherman, brought up in the rudest district of an ob-.

scure province[1].' 'In this despised region, His home
[Nazareth] was the most despised spot[2].' 'An obscure
village of despised Galilee[3],' when the very Greek text
which this scholar was editing says, πόλις, not κώμη,
i.e. *city*, not *village*. 'The roughness of its population[4].' 'The very villagers themselves spoke with a
rude and uncouth provincialism that marked them at
once as Nazarenes[5].' We have a right to ask on what
ground the statement just quoted is based. Peter
certainly was not from Nazareth, and the dialect of
any person from that city is never alluded to. 'That
obscure Galilean village[6].' One who went from the
Sea of Galilee to Judæa, 'war ein Stichblatt des Witzes
der dortigen Stammgenossen[7].' How does this writer
know that such a person became a 'butt of ridicule'?
'A little country town of proverbial insignificance,'
'the darkest district of Palestine[8].' 'The old scorn
which rested upon the Galileans in Joshua's day[9].'

These statements show the popular impression and
teaching in regard to Galilee and Nazareth. And further,
in regard to the 'poverty' and 'abject meanness' of
Christ's earthly condition, the nearly 'destitute circumstances' of Joseph and Mary, and the 'ignorance'

---

1 Conybeare and Howson, *St. Paul*, I. p. 115.
2 Delitzsch, *Jesus und Hillel*, p. 13.
3 Dr. Wordsworth on Matt. ii. 23.
4 Stanley, *Sinai and Palestine*, p. 358.
5 Lieut. Anderson in *Recovery of Jerusalem*, p. 354.
6 Plumptre, *Christ and Christendom*, p. 95.
7 Hausrath, I. p. 11.
8 Schaff, *Person of Christ*, p. 34.
9 Ritter, IV. p. 332.

and even 'immorality' of the people of Nazareth, we read a great deal in books, and hear much more in sermons from the pulpit. Numerous quotations to this effect could be given, if necessary. For instance, in Isaac Barrows' *Sermon on Patience* will be found a frightfully distressing picture of Christ's circumstances in His early years, and, indeed, during His whole earthly life, while Meyer[1] makes ἀγαθόν imply *immorality*.

But are these representations true? This is certainly a proper question to ask. These statements, appearing everywhere, and so sweeping and positive withal, ought to have some foundation, for which we propose to look.

First, as to the contempt for the Galileans on the ground of dialect, or more properly, difference of pronunciation—for we have not found any evidence showing that the 'dialect differences' so often mentioned extend beyond this slight matter. The passages in both Talmuds referring to this point are but few in number. Buxtorf, Lightfoot, and Neubauer refer to the same passages. We have noticed, and could give reasons to justify such a conclusion, that in all matters relating to Palestine the Jerusalem Talmud seems to be the more consistent and reliable. We should expect this, from the fact that it was compiled earlier than the other (A.D. 350–400), and written in the country itself. In this Talmud this whole matter of dialect is reduced to the simple statement that the doctors (of Judæa) did not distinguish between *He* and *Cheth*, nor between *Aleph* and *Ayin*—this simple statement, without comment. The Babylonian Talmud has the same. But the latter

[1] Com. on John i. 47.

(completed about A.D. 500) has, in addition, several amusing stories illustrating the peculiar pronunciation of the Galileans. The late date of the compilation of this work would damage its evidence. Where the Jerusalem Talmud is silent, the later Babylonian Talmud cannot be brought forward to show that the Jews of Jerusalem treated with contempt or ridicule their brethren of Galilee on the ground of the pronunciation of the latter. It is a very significant fact that St. Jerome, A.D. 331–422, considered himself peculiarly fortunate in obtaining a Hebrew teacher from Tiberias, because Hebrew was there spoken with such purity. After thus collecting the facts, it appears as if the doctors in the schools of the East invented certain stories in regard to the pronunciation of the Galileans (and of the Judæans as well), by 'which to amuse themselves or their pupils at the expense of their brethren in Palestine[1].

The dialect of Galilee is referred to but once in the New Testament, namely, in connection with Peter at the trial of Christ. Of this event there are four accounts[2]. The 'speech,' or peculiar pronunciation, of Peter is mentioned by Matthew only[3], for the words 'and thy speech agreeth' in Mark xiv. 70, are probably to be omitted. It is often alleged that Peter's 'speech' was alluded to by way of contempt. This passage and the one in Mark are the only evidence which Hausrath

---

[1] Lightfoot, I. pp. 170-172; Graetz, III., p. 395; Neubauer, pp. 184, 185; Buxtorf, *Lexicon*, pp. 224, 225, art. בלל; Renan, *Lang. Sémitiques*, p. 230.

[2] Matt. xxvi. 69-75; Mark xiv. 66-72; Luke xxii. 54-62; John xviii. 25-27.   [3] Matt. xxvi. 73.

produces to prove his assertion that 'a man' from the
Sea of Galilee became in Judæa,' on account of his
pronunciation, 'a butt of ridicule [1].' But no contempt
was here either expressed or implied   Peter had denied
a certain statement, and the bystanders, to justify
themselves, without any thought of ridicule or contempt,
said simply: 'Your speech reveals you to be a Galilean,'
as we have alleged (καὶ γὰρ ἡ λαλιά σου δηλόν σε ποιεῖ) [2].
Sometimes Acts ii. 7 is referred to as supporting the
view stated above.   But there could hardly be a more
unjust use of the passage.   The point of surprise on the
part of the audience was, that so few men, all coming
from the same region, should speak all the languages of
the world.   The surprise would have been great if the
speakers had all come from Greece, Italy, or Babylon.
In this case they were from Galilee.   But nothing can
be inferred from this passage which is in any way
derogatory to the character of the Galileans.   Besides
the above, there are no other passages in the New
Testament which bear upon the matter of the dialect
of Galilee.   On this point Josephus is silent—a significant fact.   Thus, neither in Josephus, the New
Testament, nor the Talmud, is there any ground, as
regards dialect, why the people of Jerusalem should
regard with contempt the inhabitants of this northern
province ; nor is there the slightest evidence that *on this
ground* the people of Jerusalem regarded the people of
Galilee with any such feeling at all.   Yet this matter of
dialect is one of the strongest arguments held up before
the popular mind to prove the existence of the alleged

[1] I. p. 11.   [2] Matt. xxvi. 73.

feeling of contempt. Further, and this fact ought to receive special emphasis, what a splendid instrument this matter of dialect would have been in the hands of the enemies of Christ, to be used against Him and His disciples! *If this difference of dialect was the occasion of any feeling between the people of the two sections, if on this account the Galileans were really laughing-stocks in Jerusalem, then what stupidity on the part of Christ's enemies not to have used this most effective means for silencing Him and counteracting His influence.* The silence of Christ's enemies is a strong argument against the supposition that *on the ground of dialect* there existed among the Jews of Jerusalem a feeling of contempt for the Galileans.

Another alleged ground is the 'religious looseness' which is supposed to have prevailed in Galilee. But we have seen that the Galileans were stricter in regard to morals than the people of Judæa, and that the former adhered more closely to the law than the latter, while the latter put *tradition* foremost. These facts speak for themselves. Another ground is, that the people of the north were a mixed race. We have shown that they are to be regarded as thoroughly Jewish. Another is that the Galileans would not be dictated to by the Doctors of Jerusalem. If this, in so far as it is fact at all, occasioned any feeling, it nowhere appears, or is even hinted at. Again, Keim makes the circumstance that John Hyrcanus sent his son Alexander Jannæus, the subsequent king, to Galilee to be brought up, imply his contempt for Galilee. Whereas the only point in this fact is that Hyrcanus wanted his son out of his sight—

in Galilee, or anywhere else, where he would not see him again. Keim presses still another fact altogether too far, when he says that 'Antipater regarded his younger son, the youngster Herod' [but he was then twenty-five!] 'as smart enough—fur tüchtig genug—to govern Galilee,' implying the very opposite of what the facts indicate, as given by Josephus. Herod was sent to Galilee because, of the two sons of Antipater, he was the more shrewd, active, and capable.

Delitzsch states the popular view as if it were a firmly established fact, instead of being, as it really is, a supposition with hardly a shadow of proof: his words are, 'The Judæans regarded the Galileans with proud contempt, just as the Greeks regarded the Bœotians, or the Parisians the people of Gascony [1]:' which we are ready to admit as soon as any evidence can be adduced in support of it. The Christians are once called 'the sect of the Nazarenes,' and alluded to as such in one other instance [2], as a sect obnoxious to the Jews; but in neither case is any contempt implied for Galilee or Nazareth. In John vii. 41 all that is meant is that the people universally expected Christ to come from Bethlehem, and not from Galilee. As to the statement in John vii. 52, it is possible that the speakers referred to *the* prophet alluded to in verse 40, and also in chap. vi. 14. But if they really meant that no prophet ever came from Galilee, they stated what they knew to be false, that is, supposing that they possessed even the commonest knowledge of their own history. There are besides the above no other passages in the New Testament which

---

[1] *Jesus und Hillel*, p. 13.   [2] Acts xxiv. 5; xxviii. 22

bear at all upon our subject, except John i. 46, Nathanael's words, which will be considered later.

The grounds mentioned above, on which it is claimed by some that a feeling of contempt for the Galileans was based, are all suppositions of later times. We can readily imagine that, on the part of Jerusalem and its inhabitants, there was a feeling of superiority to Galilee and the Galileans. But that such a feeling (of the existence of which at all we have no proof) ever amounted to contempt, or even to sectional jealousy or prejudice, there is not the slightest evidence in any of the great authorities, namely, the New Testament, Josephus, and the Talmud. Yet, if such a feeling really existed, it must have appeared somewhere. On this point, the following summary of facts will be significant :—

1. On a certain occasion of distress in the northern province, mentioned in 1 Mac. v. 14–23, the Maccabees, though belonging to the tribe of Judah, rallied nobly for the defence of the Galileans—their brethren of the north. There is no trace of sectional feeling here.

2. In A.D. 51 the Galileans were attacked at Ginæa by the Samaritans, while the former were on their way to a feast at Jerusalem. 'When the assassination was reported at Jerusalem, the populace were thrown into a state of confusion, and, deserting the festival, hurried to Samaria,' to revenge the outrage committed against their brethren of the north. Here is the very opposite of sectional feeling between Judæa and Galilee.

3. Had such a feeling existed, it would have cropped out at the great feasts, the common occasions for the display of ill-feeling or mad passions, if any existed,

towards any person or party. But a friendly feeling always appears ; for,

4. At the outbreak at Pentecost (May 31, in B.C. 4) after the death of Herod, Galileans, Idumæans, men from Jericho and Peræa, join with the Judæans in an attack upon Sabinus and the Roman troops, and apparently there is the greatest harmony among the people of the different sections.

5. During the governorship of Herod, and afterwards during his reign (from the time he was twenty-five until he was seventy), and during the long reign of Antipas (forty-three years), and the short reign of Agrippa I., and the governorship of Josephus, in all the events which transpired during these years, there is no trace of sectional feeling or jealousy.

6. The opposite of such a feeling is indicated by the visiting back and forth of the Scribes and Pharisees in Christ's time.

7. In the Jewish war, the greatest harmony prevails, for the most part, between Galilee and Judæa.

8. The silence of the enemies of Christ.

9. The silence, on this subject, of the New Testament, of Josephus, and of the Talmud. If Galilee was 'a despised province,' if 'the Galileans were looked upon with contempt,' ought there not to be hints of such facts *somewhere?*

XVIII.

NAZARETH, ITS CHARACTER AND PROBABLE SIZE;
ORIGIN OF THE NAME; NOT SO ISOLATED AS IS
SUPPOSED.

IN regard to Nazareth, some have apparently felt that
they were honouring Christ in proportion as they were
able to make His earthly home appear insignificant
and mean. The pictures which have been drawn of
the 'meanness' of Nazareth, and of the 'poverty' of
Christ's family, are as distressing as they are untruth-
ful. It is a question whether the words of Nathanael
have not been misunderstood. The Greek can be
translated easily; but we refer to the *spirit* of the words.
In common with all the pious at that time, Nathanael
expected Christ to appear at Bethlehem. 'The passage
in Micah v. 2[1] left no doubt in the minds of the Sanhedrin
as to the birthplace of the Messiah,' i.e. it could occur
only at Bethlehem. So Nathanael believed with the
rest. Consequently, any one who should announce that
He had appeared elsewhere, would at once be said to be
mistaken. This is a striking case, we think, where too
strict adherence to the letter does violence to the sentiments of the speaker and to the well-known facts of the

[1] Comp. Matt. ii. 6.

H

time. Nathanael in his surprise said only, 'The great good which we expect cannot come from Nazareth, because Scripture has declared that He must come from Bethlehem.' Thus the words of Nathanael are best explained. Thus, also, we do not make this man whom the lips of the Saviour declared to be 'an Israelite indeed, in whom is no guile,' guilty of cherishing, at that very moment, a contemptible spirit of local jealousy. Those who infer from the τι ἀγαθόν of Nathanael that Nazareth was an immoral place, found their assumption on a mere fancy, which is supported by not a single fact, and, indeed, is contradicted by all that we know of the place and people.

Those who claim that Nathanael meant to contrast the insignificance of the place with the greatness of the Messiah are equally wrong; for this could have been said of Bethlehem, where He was expected to appear, or, if one chose, of even Jerusalem itself, had He appeared there.

It is often said that Nazareth is not mentioned in the Old Testament or in Josephus; implying that hence it must have been an insignificant place. As to Josephus, he speaks only of those places which he has occasion to mention; and out of the two hundred and four cities and villages of Galilee he names but about forty. Neither is Capernaum mentioned in the Old Testament or the Apocrypha, and but once (perhaps not that) in Josephus. Yet we know it was a place of importance.

As to the origin of the name 'Nazareth,' no one can decide definitely. At the same time, one explanation may be found to be more probable than any of the

others. We reject that which derives it from נָזַר
consecrated or *devoted* to God. Also, that which makes
it come from נוֹצְרִי, *my Saviour*. Likewise the very
popular one for which Hengstenberg, in his *Christology*,
labours, who derives it from נֵצֶר, a *shoot* or *sprout*. Isa.
xi. 1 is the only place where נֵצֶר is used with reference
to Christ. But if the name were to contain a reference
to the Messiah as a *sprout* or *branch* of David, it should
have been some form of צֶמַח, the usual word for
'branch,' and which is supposed to have direct reference to the Messiah. The explanation of Hengstenberg
(and held by many others) is very improbable; for is
it likely that a place would be named from a certain
prophecy, and from a certain word in that prophecy,
years, and perhaps centuries, before that prophecy was
fulfilled? A town could hardly have failed to have
existed on so eligible a site from very early times. The
hill just behind the present town is spoken of by every
traveller as commanding one of the finest prospects in
Palestine. It could not have wanted a name, any more
than Hermon, Tabor, or Gilboa. Mountains in every
country are frequently named from some peculiarity of
their own. We have long had the impression, confirmed
since we stood on the hill itself, that the name of the
town and the hill must be intimately connected, or
perhaps identical. If we had the name of the latter,
we should know that of the former. We have already
shown that to the New Testament writers this place
was a πόλις, and never a κώμη (i.e. 'city,' not 'village'),
and hence of size and importance, in spite of modern

commentaries and sermons, which insist on its insignificance.   Keim puts the probable number of its inhabitants
'at ten thousand souls, at least.'   But if we receive the
statement of Josephus, before quoted, as to the towns
and cities of Galilee, we may suppose the number of its
inhabitants to have reached fifteen or twenty thousand.
We have, then, a mountain 'city' of some importance
and of considerable antiquity.   We have the hill at the
back of the town, commanding that wonderful prospect.
This hill must have had a name. We have the word נָצַר,
to behold, to see, to look, and then *to watch, to guard*.   In the
latter sense (*watch* or *guard*) it is often used in Hebrew
(perhaps a dozen times).   We have נוֹצֵר, *one guarding;*
and נוֹצְרָה, *one guarding*, respectively masculine and
feminine   נְצוּרָה, construct נְצוּרַת, *one guarded* (fem.)
If Nazareth is from נְצוּרָה, it would signify the *watched*
or *guarded one* (fem.), i.e., the hill-top seen or beheld
from afar.   If from נוֹצְרָה, we have the one *guarding* or
watching (fem.), i.e., the hill which overlooks a vast
region—in this case land and sea—and thus guards it.
Both these facts are true of the Nazareth-hill.   In the
oldest Greek manuscripts both the forms Nazara and
Nazareth appear.   One cannot read the article in Furst's
Hebrew and Chaldee Lexicon, natzar—although he does
not allude to the question here discussed—without being
impressed with the idea that if the word *Nazareth* is to
be derived from the Hebrew at all, it must come from
this root, and have the signification which we have given
and adopted.

The view of Hitzig, as given by Tobler, making the

name refer to some *helping* goddess of the old Canaan-
itish times, we cannot adopt. The view above presented
is one which seemed to us most plausible, and which we
had written out and adopted before we had seen Keim's
first volume. We are gratified to find that he connects
the city with the hill as to the origin of its name : and he
gives, in substance, the view we have advocated. We
submit this as the most natural explanation of the origin
of the word 'Nazareth.' It cannot be charged, as every
one of the others can, with being 'far-fetched.' It
relieves the name from any theological or prophetical
character. If it was to have a theological or a prophetical
import, it was unnatural, to say the least, to derive it
from נֵצֶר instead of from צֶמַה. נֵצֶר is used but once
in any such connection ; while צֶמַה is used many times.

Much is said about the 'absolute seclusion' of
Nazareth as the home of Christ. In regard to this
point the following facts are important: 1. The probable size of the place, as before mentioned. 2. The
Nazareth-hill was seen and known throughout all
that province, in Samaria also, and by the sailors
on the Mediterranean Sea. 3. Its distance from other
places—three short days' journey from Jerusalem ;
about six hours from Ptolemais, the port at which
news and merchandise from Rome first reached
Palestine (as regards the early receiving of news
and merchandise from Rome, Galilee had the advantage of Jerusalem and Judæa) ; about five hours
from the Sea of Galilee; two or three hours from
Endor and Nain; two hours from Mount Tabor ;

about one hour and a half from Cana of Galilee;
also one hour and a half from Sepphoris, which
before Christ's time was the capital of Galilee, and
even remained so until Herod Antipas built Tiberias,
in A.D. 28.   4. Doubtless, roads led out from Nazareth
in Christ's time in every direction, the same as to-day.
'The main road for the land traffic between Egypt and
the interior of Asia must have been the great highway
leading past Gaza,' through the mountains at Megiddo,
and across the Plain of Esdraelon, passing Nazareth
near the foot of Tabor, and thence on to the Northern
Jordan and Damascus. If the caravan routes from
Tyre and Sidon passed to the north of Nazareth,
that from Ptolemais to Damascus would no doubt
make Capernaum, if not Tiberias, on its line, and
hence would pass very near to Nazareth.   5. Its
proximity to the capital of the province, Sepphoris—
which is in sight from the Nazareth-hill—and to
other large cities, and its nearness to the great caravan
routes of commerce, would bring it into constant intercourse with the centres of business and news (Ptolemais,
Capernaum, Tiberias, Scythopolis, Sepphoris, and of
course Damascus), and give it, in this respect, very
important advantages, which they should consider well
who insist upon the 'great obscurity and isolation of
the place'—a supposition wholly gratuitous, as is seen
by the facts now presented.

After what we have thus far learned of Galilee, it
sounds strange enough to read, especially from an
eminent author, that 'Jesus grew up among a people
seldom, or only contemptuously, named by the ancient

classics, and subjected, at the time, to the yoke of a foreign oppressor ; in a remote and conquered province of the Roman empire ; in the darkest district of Palestine ; in a country town of proverbial insignificance ; in poverty and manual labour; in the obscurity of a carpenter's shop ; far away from universities, academies, libraries, and literary or polished society,' &c.

In regard to 'manual labour,' it should be remembered that in Christ's time it was a disgrace *not* to labour. The most eminent teachers engaged regularly in 'manual labour.' How far must Christ have gone to have found 'universities, academies, and libraries'? They certainly did not exist in Jerusalem. The whole paragraph gives an entirely wrong impression in regard to the city and province where Christ lived, and as to the circumstances of His early life. The *colouring* of this picture is false.

XIX

SUMMARY OF RESULTS: GALILEE PROVIDENTIALLY FITTED FOR THE FIRST RECEPTION OF CHRIST AND HIS GOSPEL.

AFTER the careful review now closed, we feel justified in saying that Galilee at the time of Christ was one of the finest and most fertile portions of the earth. Stretching from the Mediterranean on the west to the Jordan and the sweet-watered Merom and Gennesareth on the east; abounding in springs, rivers, and lakes— among which its one hallowed sea was the gem and pride of the whole country, as it is for ever dear to Christian hearts; possessing a rare and delightful climate, and scenery of great variety and beauty; its surface never dull or monotonous, but wonderfully varied by plains and valleys, gentle slopes and terraced hills, deep ravines and bold peaks, naturally fortified eminences and giant mountains; its soil naturally fertile. but forced by skilful husbandry to the highest state of productiveness, until this province was noted for the perfection and abundance of its fruits; Galilee thus possessed features of richness and beauty rarely if ever combined in so small a country in all the world besides. The surface of the country was covered with wealthy cities and flourishing towns, and crossed in many directions by her 'way of the sea' and other great thoroughfares, which were thronged with the caravans of commerce. Its agriculture and fisheries, wine and oil trade, and other industries, were in the most flourishing condition, being managed with energy and skill by a people who knew well how to use to advantage the resources of their highly favoured country. Its synagogues and other public buildings were built often in splendid style and at great expense. Here money was abundant, and easily raised either for taxes, heavy tributes, military affairs, or for costly dwellings and palaces. Here all matters pertaining to the synagogical service and to the instruction of children were faithfully attended to, and here were found teachers, learned men, missionaries, poets, and patriots of the highest order.

In regard to the character of the Galileans, it is claimed that gold and dross were lying side by side. But even those who discover in them a great deal of exterior roughness are compelled to admit that beneath this rough surface they possessed a fund of strength and talent which entitled them to the highest regard. But much of a positive character can be said in their praise. Their patriotism in national emergencies ; their enthusiastic loyalty to their country's interests ; their general adherence to the law of Moses in preference to tradition, which ruled and hampered the public mind in Jerusalem ; their interests in the Temple and its solemn feasts ; their deep-seated and inspiring hope, which looked with steadfast gaze towards the future— ' waiting for the redemption of Israel,'—these things show that the Jews of the north, at least equally with, and perhaps far beyond, those who dwelt beneath the very shadow of the Temple, maintained within themselves, in their integrity, some of the noblest traits of the Hebrew nation.

But farther, we find the Galileans to have been a moral, intelligent, industrious, and enterprising people, possessed of vigorous minds and healthy bodies—'healthy as their own climate and cheerful as their own sky,'—a people familiar with their own law and history, and not wanting in the finest poetical spirit; with the disposition and ability to appreciate in the main the teachings of Christ; a people among whom were found most devoted men. 'Israelites indeed'; among whom also devotion to the national idea reached its highest development, till at last they rose, a solid wall of patriot hearts, to be crushed by the all-conquering power of Rome; both country and people, one may say with truth, fitly chosen of God as the training-place of those men—Master and disciples—who were to move the world; the proper soil in which first to plant the seeds of that truth which was destined, ere long, to be spoken by eloquent lips in the pulpits of Cæsarea, Antioch, Constantinople, and Rome.

LIST OF AUTHORITIES QUOTED.

———•———

THE following is a list of the authors we have consulted in preparing the present work. In a large number of instances these authors are quoted as authorities for isolated statements. This remark is made lest any one might suppose that the volumes referred to contained a detailed account of Galilee, which is not the case.

ALFORD. New Testament.

ARNAUD. La Palestine ancienne et moderne, 1 vol. Paris, 1868.

BURTON AND DRAKE. Unexplored Syria, 2 vols. London, 1872.

BUXTORF. Lex. Chald. Tal. et Rab., new edit. by Fischer.

CHIARINI. Le Talmud, 2 vols. Leipzig, 1831.

CONYBEARE AND HOWSON. Life and Epistles of St. Paul, 2 vols. in 1. New York, 1869.

DELITZSCH. Handwerkerleben zur Zeit Jesu. Erlangen, 1868. Also, Jesus und Hillel. *Ibid.*, 1867.

DERENBOURG. Histoire de la Palestine, d'après des Thalmuds et les autres sources Rabbiniques, 1 vol. Paris, 1867.

EWALD. History of Israel, Eng. trans. London, 1869, *et seq.*

FURRER. Wanderungen durch Palästina, 1 vol. Zürich, 1865.

FÜRST. Kultur- und Literaturgeschichte der Juden in Asien, 1 vol. Leipzig, 1849.

GEIGER. Urschrift und Uebersetzungen der Bibel, 1 vol. Breslau, 1857.

GFRÖRER.   The first vol. of his Das Jahrhundert des Heils.
      Stuttgart, 1838.

GRAETZ.   The third vol. of his Geschichte der Juden.   Edition
      of Leipzig, 1856.

———— Sinai et Golgotha, ou les origines du Judaisme et du
      Christianisme, 1 vol.   Paris, 1867.

GROVE.   In Smith's Bible Dictionary.

HAUSRATH.   Neutestamentliche Zeitgeschichte.   Vol. i., Hei-
      delberg, 1868; vol. ii., *ibid.*, 1872.

HERZFELD.   Geschichte des Volkes Israel, 3 vols.   Braun-
      schweig, 1847, *et seq.*

JAHN.   Bib. Archæology, 3rd edit., 1 vol.   Andover, 1832.

JOSEPHUS.   Edit. Dindorf, pub. Didot, 2 vols.   Paris, 1845,
      1847.   Trans. of Antiquities by Whiston.   Trans. of
      the Wars by Traill, edited by Isaac Taylor, 2 vols.
      London, 1851.

JOST.   Gesch. des Judenthums und seiner Secten, 3 vols.
      Leipzig, 1857, *et seq.*   Also, vol. ii. of his Gesch der
      Israeliten, edit. Berlin, 1821.

KEIM.   Geschichte Jesu von Nazara, 3 vols.   Zürich, 1867–
      1872.

KENRICK.   Phœnicia, 1 vol.   London, 1855.

KITTO.   Cyclop. Bib. Lit., edit. by W. L. Alexander, 3rd
      edition, 3 vols.   1866.

LEWIN   Fasti Sacri, 1 vol.   London, 1865.

LIGHTFOOT.   Horæ Hebraicæ, edit. by Robert Gandell, in
      4 vols.   Oxford, 1859.

LUTTERBECK.   Die neutestamentlichen Lehrbegriffe, 2 vols.
      Mainz, 1852.

MADDEN.   Jewish Coinage, 1 vol.   London, 1864.

MERIVALE.   History of the Romans under the Empire, 7 vols.
      New York, 1871.

MEYER.   Commentary on the New Testament.

MILMAN. History of the Jews, 3 vols. London, 1866.

MUNK. Palestine, 1 vol. Paris, 1863.

NEUBAUER. La Géographie du Talmud, 1 vol. Paris, 1868.

PALESTINE EXPLORATION FUND. The Recovery of Jerusalem, 1 vol. Also, by the same, Our Work in Palestine, 1 vol.

PLINY.

PLUMPTRE. Christ and Christendom, 1 vol. London, 1867.

PORTER. Handbook for Syria and Palestine. Also, Giant Cities of Bashan, 1 vol.

RAUMER (Von). Palästina, 1 vol. Leipzig, 1860.

RAWLINSON. Ancient Monarchies, 3 vols.

RELAND. Palæstina. 1714.

RENAN. Histoire Générale des Langues Sémitiques, 1 vol. Paris, 1863.

—— Life of Jesus. Eng. trans., 1 vol. New York, 1871.

RITTER. Geography of Palestine. Trans. in 4 vols. by W. L. Gage.

ROBINSON. Biblical Researches. 2nd edit., 3 vols. Boston, 1860.

SCHAFF. The Person of Christ. New York, 1866.

SCHNECKENBURGER. Neutestamentliche Zeitgeschichte, 1 vol. Frankfurt am Main, 1862.

SCHWARTZ. Das heilige Land, 1 vol. Frankfurt am Main, 1852.

SMITH. Dictionary of the Bible.

STANLEY. Sinai and Palestine, 1 vol. Also, Jewish Church, 2 vols.

STRABO.

TACITUS.

TALMUD. Jerusalem.

—— Babylonian.

THOMSON. The Land and the Book, 2 vols. New York, 1859.

TOBLER. Nazareth, 1 vol. Berlin, 1868.
TRISTRAM. Natural History of the Bible, 1 vol. London,
    1868. Also, The Land of Israel: a Journal, &c., 1 vol.
    London, 1866.
VAN DE VELDE. Syria and Palestine, 2 vols. London, 1854.
WEBER AND HOLTZMANN. Geschichte des Volkes Israel, 2
    vols. Leipzig, 1867.
WILLIAMS. The Holy City, 2 vols. London, 1849.
WILSON. Lands of the Bible, 2 vols. Edinburgh, 1847.

We would refer to the notes of Isaac Taylor, in his edition of
Traill's Josephus' Wars, as very important. The little book of
Schneckenburger is comprehensive and clear. Lewin's work
is of great value.

Neubauer's Géographie is a most serviceable volume. Dr.
J. Morgenstern published, in 1870 (two pamphlets, Berlin), a
severe review of it, entitled, *Die französische Academie und die
' Geographie des Talmuds,'* which we have used in connection
with Neubauer's work. On the other hand, Dr. M. A. Levy,
in the *Zeitschrift der D. M. Gesellschaft*, 1869, p. 699, and Dr.
Geiger, in the *Jüdische Zeitschrift für Wissenschaft und Leben*,
1869, p 62, *et seq.*, both praise Neubauer's *Géographie*, as a
work of great merit. Hausrath is always fresh and suggestive.
We can, with much justice, call him the German Stanley.
Keim's is a vast work, and characterised by fulness and
richness.

Graetz's *Geschichte* is likewise of great importance ; but sometimes his conclusions are too hasty and his spirit too partisan
for the candid historian.

INDEX.

—•—

Achabara, celebrated for pheasants, 39.
Adiabene, Eleazar, a Jewish missionary in, 91.
Agriculture of Galilee, 33.
  among the Galileans, 70, 71.
Agrippa and Berenice, steward of, robbed, and outbreak which followed, 64.
Agrippa I., see under Herod.
Agrippa II., see under Herod.
Alexander, son of Aristobulus, defeated near Mount Tabor by Gabinius, 55.
Alexander, a Jewish philosopher of Alexandria, said to be from Paneas, 95.
Alexander Jannæus calls Galilee his fatherland, 95.
Alexandra, queen, Pharisees rise to power during her reign, 83.
  her character, 90.
Alexandria, fish of its lake similar to those in a spring near Gennesareth, 24.
  glass-shops of, 42.
Amphitheatre at Jerusalem, 90.
Andrew, from Bethsaida, 51, 97.
Anna the prophetess, from Asher, 95.
Antioch, contribution sent from, to the poor Christians in Judæa, 100.
Antiochus the Great, battle of, near Mount Tabor, 54.
  at Paneas, 56.

Antipater, father of Herod the Great, raising money for Cassius, 101.
Antony gives Cæsarea Philippi to Cleopatra, 58.
  his lust, 90.
Aqueducts, remains of ancient, 32.
Arabah, grain merchants meeting at, 40.
Arabs aid the Romans in the Jewish war, 75.
Arbela, a stronghold, 51.
  fortified caves, 51.
  refuge of robbers, 51.
  celebrated for cloth, 40.
  home of Nitai, a doctor of the Mishna, 95.
Archelaus, ethnarch of Judæa, 12, 13.
  married his brother's widow, 88.
  this conduct condemned, 88.
  banished by Augustus, 13.
Archives of Galilee kept at Sepphoris, 55.
Aristobulus II. found his best soldiers in Galilee, 73.
Army, large, raised by Josephus in Galilee, 63.
  heroic deeds of the Galilean, in Jerusalem, 73.
  Roman, splendid discipline of, 74.
  number of, in Jewish war, 75.
  contrast between, and the Galilean, 75.
  a part of the, supported in winter quarters in Galilee, 100.

Arsenal of Herod Antipas at Sepphoris, 55.
vast collection of arms in, 65.
Asher, oil production of, 35.
part taken by, in the pursuit of
the Midianites, 76
Athronges sets himself up for a
king in Judæa, on the death of
Herod the Great, 81.
Augustus, emperor, decree of, against
lofty houses, 54

Babylon, costly products of, passing
through Galilee, 100.
Balinas, an old name for Banias, 55
Banias, a well-watered region, 30
fertility about, 39
Barak and Deborah rallied their
forces on Mount Tabor, 76
victory over the Canaanites, 94.
song celebrating the same, 93.
Barbadoes, island of, inhabitants
to a square mile, 20.
Bar Cochab, rebellion under, against
Rome, 65
Barley furnished by Solomon to
Hiram, 37.
Bashan full of ruined towns, 66
Battle-field of Joshua at Lake
Merom, 56
of Antiochus the Great at Paneas,
56.
at Mount Tabor, 55.
of Deborah and Barak, 76.
of Gamala, 49.
of Gadara, 60.
of Japha, 74.
of Jotapata, 60, 74
of Gabinius at Mount Tabor, 55
Battle-fields of the Jewish nation,
some of the most remark-
able were in Galilee, 76
a bloody on the Lake of Tiberias,
46.
Belus, the river, glass-making connected with, 29
furnished sand for the glass-shops
of the world, 42.
Berytus, lofty houses at, 54.

Beth-arbel. See Arbela
Bethlehem, Christ expected to appear at, 110, 113, 114
Bethmaus, near Tiberias, its synagogue, 48.
Bethsaida, the eastern, meaning of
the name, 44.
Bethsaida, rebuilt by Herod Philip,
and called Julias, 50
Philip buried there, 50
scene of one of Christ's miracles
near, 50
Bethsaida, the western, 51.
called Bethsaida in Galilee, 51.
home of Philip, Andrew, and
Peter, 51.
probably of Zebedee, James, and
John, 51.
was a city, 51.
Christ intimately connected with,
51.
character of, 105.
Bethshean, the 'gate of Paradise,'
39.
fertility of, 39
population, 54.
Bible-study, a revival of, during the
reign of Alexandra, 84.
Biram, warm springs at, 31.
Birket Israil in Jerusalem, pottery
found there, 41.
Boys, education of, devolved upon
the father, 85.
Brass shops of Tyre, 42
praised by Homer, 42.
Bridge over the Jordan below the
Lake of Tiberias, 49
on the main route to the east, 49
Building in Christ's time, a great
amount of public, 70
costly, of Herod Antipas at Tiberias, 52, 53
Burying-ground found by workmen
when Tiberias was built, 53.

Cabul, meaning of the term as used
by Hiram not yet explained, 16
Caboul, a town in Galilee, sends
treasures to Jerusalem, 100.

Cæsarea on the sea-coast, Herod Agrippa I. dies at, 13, 58.

Cæsarea, Jews in, outnumber the Greeks, 98.

Cæsarea Philippi belongs to Galilee, 19.

Jews at, cannot obtain pure oil, 36.

had several names, 58.

a variety of masters, 58.

adorned by Herod the Great, 57.

enlarged by Herod Philip, 57.

marble temple at, 57.

castle, 57.

seat of ancient idol-worship, 55.

situation, 56.

Titus visits and celebrates games at, 59.

Agrippa II. entertains Vespasian at, 59.

chequered history of, 59, 60.

visited by Christ, 59.

scene of transfiguration near, 59.

Christ's conversation with His disciples at, 60.

road leading eastward from, 57.

Caius attempts to erect his statue in the temple at Jerusalem, 88.

Caligula, the emperor, gives Cæsarea Philippi to Herod Agrippa I., 58.

Cana of Galilee, 54, 60.

Josephus at, 60.

Capellus, Julius, a leader in Tiberias, 96.

Capernaum, wheat of, 39.

wheat fields, 51.

Josephus wounded near, 49.

tax-gatherers, 52.

custom-house, 52.

garrison, 52.

schools and synagog e, 52.

importance of, as compared with Tiberias, 52.

the home of Christ, 52.

on the road from Egypt to Damascus, 52.

Christ's rebuke of, 52.

a centre of news, 100.

Capernaum, a place of luxury, 100.

Christ called 'a gluttonous man' at, 100.

learned men there from all parts of the country, 86.

not mentioned in the Old Testament, 114.

Carmel once belonged to Galilee, 19.

Cassius sold the inhabitants of Tarichæa as slaves, 48.

raising men and money in Syria, 101.

four cities reduced to slavery by, 101.

Cattle, Galilee raised more grain than, 25, 39.

Census of Tribes which occupied Galilee in time of Joshua, 64.

Chananyah, Kefr, 19.

production of pottery, 40, 41.

proverb with regard to, 40.

Character, Jewish, permanence of, how maintained, 69, 70.

Chorazin, meaning of name, 44.

wheat and wheat fields of, 39, 51.

Christ's rebuke of, 51, 52.

character of, 100.

Christ, misrepresentations of His home and circumstances in early life, 10, 106, 118.

was expected to appear in Bethlehem, 110, 113, 114.

did he ever visit Tiberias? 53.

practised and encouraged manual labour, 71.

not an Essene, as sometimes alleged, 38.

generally well received in Galilee, 87, 91.

cold reception in Jerusalem, 87.

could hardly have planted Himself in Judæa, 92.

called a 'gluttonous man,' 100.

rebukes Bethsaida, Chorazin, and Capernaum, 52, 100.

at Cæsarea Philippi, 59.

scene of His transfiguration, 59.

I

Christ, conversation with His disciples at, 60.

constant reference to natural objects, 9

must not study, exclusively, from the spiritual side, 9

contempt of, for tradition, 87.

familiarity of, with the Scriptures, 87.

silence of the enemies of, bearing on the dialect of Galilee, 109.

Galilee providentially chosen as the scene of His appearance and ministry, 120.

Christians called the sect of the Nazarenes, 110.

Cicero thought manual labour degrading, 71.

Cities and villages of Galilee, sixty-nine mentioned in Joshua's time, 18

sixteen in Naphtali were fortified, 18

number of, mentioned by Josephus, 17, 54.

difficulty in locating those mentioned by name, 17.

Josephus' statement examined, 63, et seq.

commanding situations of some of the, 54, 55.

in the East packed with people, 66.

about the Sea of Galilee, 51.

Clay, the dark preferred for pottery, 40.

Cleopatra, Cæsarea Philippi once belonged to, 58.

Climate of the Plain of Gennesareth, 24, 25.

of Galilee a perpetual spring, 22.

supposed effect on the character of the Galileans, 83

Cloth made at Arbela, 40.

Cœle-Syria given to Herod the Great, 101

ommerce, routes of, through Galilee, 71.

Commerce, inland, 100

of the Phœnicians affecting Galilee, 41.

Compsus, a prominent man in Tiberias, 96.

Contrasts between affairs in Galilee and those in Judæa, 79, 80.

strange historical, in the Holy Land, 59

at Cæsarea Philippi, 59

Corinth, inhabitants of Tarichæa sent by Nero to work on the canal at, 48

Council of Tiberias, size of, 53.

Courage, Galileans noted for, 71, et seq.

Crassus robbed the temple at Jerusalem, 98, 101.

Crete, Jews in, numerous and wealthy, 98.

Crispus, a prominent man in Tiberias, 96.

Cumanus, Cæsarea Philippi once governed by, 58.

did the Jews a favour, 80.

negligence of, 78.

Cuspius Fadus, Cæsarea Philippi once governed by, 58.

Customs, various, respecting which the people of Galilee were more strict than those of Judæa, 88

Cyprus, copper mines of, under the care of Herod the Great, 102.

Deborah, a prophetess, perhaps from Issachar, 94.

and Barak rallied their forces at Mount Tabor, 76

Decapolis, the region of, full of towns, 66.

Scythopolis the largest city of, 61

Dew about Mount Tabor important to vegetation, 30.

Dialect of the Galileans, question discussed, 107, et seq.

Distance from Nazareth to certain places, 117.

Divorce, law of, among the Jews,

not the same for men as for women, 88.

Drusilla marries Felix, 80.

Dyers, shops of, at Magdala, 40.
important class at Tyre and Sidon, 42.

Education among the Galileans, 82, *et seq.*

Eleazar, Jewish Missionary to Adiabene, 91.
his thorough style of preaching, 91.
was from Galilee, 95.

Eleazar, son of Jairus, obstinate resistance of, to Rome, 96.
perished at Masada, 96.

Elephants used in the Battle of Paneas under Antiochus the Great, 56.

Elijah, laboured in Galilee, 95.

Elisha, his home in Issachar, 95.

Elkosh, the home of the prophet Nahum, 95.

Elon, a judge in Israel, from Zebulun, 94.

Emmaus reduced to slavery on account of tax by Cassius, 102.

Engines of War, large number of, in siege of Jotapata, 74.

Essene, Christ not an, as alleged, 38.

Essenes renounced the use of oil, 38.
considered it defiling, 38.

Euphrates, the Jews on the, 98.

Exploration Fund, English Palestine, map of, reliable for modern topography, 18.

Farmers of Galilee industrious and skilful, 25.

Fatherland, what a noble race will accomplish when struggling for, 73, 75.

Feasts in Jerusalem, why fruits of Gennesareth not found at, 25.
fish provided for, from the Sea of Galilee, 44.

Felix, treatment of the Jews by, 80.

Fertility of Galilee, 22, *et seq.*

Figs of the Plain of Gennesareth, 24, 26.

Fîk, the site of Hippos, 49.

Fish in a spring near Gennesareth, like those in the Lake of Alexandria, 24.

Fish, clean and unclean, Jews distinguish between, 44.
Christ's reference to, 44.

Fisheries of the Sea of Galilee, 43-45.

Flax extensively used in Galilee, 43.

Flowers of Galilee, 26.

Foreign influence, effect of, on the Jewish character, 69-71.
not so great as alleged, 71.

Forests in Galilee, 27.

Fortress, on Mount Tabor, 54.

Fruits reach perfection in Galilee, 25.

Gabara, an important city of Galilee, 54.

Gabatha, an important city of Galilee, 54.

Gabinius defeats Alexander, son of Aristobulus, at Mount Tabor, 55.
five councils established by, 61.

Gadara, connection of, with Galilee, 54.
a Greek city, 70.
warm springs at, 31.
its citizens fight at Tarichæa, 60.
taken by Vespasian, 60.
the inhabitants of, massacred, 60.

Galileans, character of, 68, *et seq.*
a Jewish people, 68.
somewhat influenced by neighbouring people, 68.
chiefly agriculturists, 70.
industry and enterprise among, 71.
estimate of manual labour, 71.
some friendly intercourse be-

tween, and the Samaritans, 79.

Galileans, once attacked by the latter at Ginæa, 78, 111.

poetical talent developed among, 93.

reasons why they should be honoured by the Jewish nation, 104

dialect of, question discussed,106.

stories invented in the schools of the East as to the pronunciation of, 107.

their ancestors eminent for bravery, 76.

the first to suffer in the great invasions from the East, 76

defended by the Maccabees, 111.

wonderful heroism of, in the struggle with Rome, 76

hardest fighting of the war done by, 75

number killed in one year, 75.

conduct praised by Vespasian and Titus, 75.

noble record of, 72.

devotion to their rulers, 72.

never charged with cowardice, 72

how to be judged in the Jewish war when matched with the veterans of Rome, 73, 74

vain hope of, in this war, 74.

to some degree independent of Jerusalem, 86

more cosmopolitan in feeling than the people of Judæa, 70

surprising that they were not more affected by foreign influence, 70

freer and better religious life among, than in Judæa, 87

great respect for law and order, 77, et seq

assertions to the contrary are without foundation, 77.

chief concern of, was for reputation, 89.

religion among, 82, et seq.

zeal for the law of Moses, 82, 109.

Galileans, not given to superstition, as alleged, 83.

education among, 82, 83.

how they regarded tradition, 109

superior morals of, 109.

patriotism and intelligence of, 121

summary of character of, 122.

appreciating the teaching of Christ, 122.

Galilee, and Galilee of the Gentiles, meaning of the terms, 15.

Josephus divides, into Upper and Lower, 19.

the Talmud makes three divisions, 19.

limits of, vary, 19

what it embraced, 17.

difficulty in tracing its boundaries, 17.

extent of, 19

densely populated, 20.

inhabitants to a square mile, 20

example of other countries, 20.

popular representations of, not correct, 10.

fertility of, at the time of Christ, 24.

one of the gardens of the world, 10.

a well-watered country, 28, et seq.

lakes, 28

Tiberias, 28

Merom, 28

Gennesareth said to be the special delight of Jehovah, 28.

water-brooks, 23.

Moses' testimony, 23.

Renan's praise, 23.

testimony of Josephus, 23

Dr. Zeller's testimony, 26.

astonishing fruitfulness of, 22

a scene of great activity, 22.

fine climate, 22

diversified scenery, 22.

natural attractions, 104

supplies furnished by, to Solomon's palace, 27

to the Phœnicians, 29.

Galilee, present productions, 27.

Alexander Jannæus, when a boy, sent to, to be brought up, 109.

Josephus military governor of, 63.

contrast between the manner in which it was governed and Judæa, 14.

enjoyed quiet and prosperity during reigns of Herod the Great and Herod Antipas, 79.

general character of its inhabitants, 104.

prophets, judges, and famous men of, 94, *et seq.*

character of its learned men, 87.

how regarded by the people of Judæa, 104, *et seq.*

influences existed in, which tended to broaden the mind, 87.

was there sectional feeling between, and Judæa? 109.

advantage over Judæa in various industries, 38.

affected by Phœnicia, 41–44.

struggles of, with Rome, 74.

carried on the war alone during the first year, 73.

numbers killed in, during the war, 67.

Romans proud of the conquest of, 75.

cost of their victory great, 75.

supports a portion of the Roman army, 100.

wealth and material prosperity of, 98, *et seq.*

noted cities and towns of, 48–61.

its prosperous cities indicate wealth, 100.

misrepresentations of the character of, 105, 106.

summary of results, 120, *et seq.*

Christ not expected to appear in, 110.

divinely chosen as the scene of Christ's appearance and ministry, 120.

no previous work covering the ground of the present volume, 10.

Galilee, the Sea of, its shores covered with towns, 20, 23, 48.

praised by the Rabbis, 23.

fine fishing-ground, 43.

free to all, 44.

fish from, carried to distant markets, 44.

a focus of life and activity, 46, 47.

ships and boats on, 46.

merchants crossing the, 46.

pleasure parties, 46.

ships at Tarichæa, 46.

bloody sea fight at Tarichæa, 46.

see also Gennesareth, the Sea of.

Gamala, meaning of the name, 49.

the Talmud reckons it belongs to Galilee, 19.

situation, 49.

view from, 49.

strength of, 50.

besieged by Agrippa II., 50.

attacked by Vespasian, 50.

heroic defence of, 74.

at last subdued, 50.

Gamaliel, the great teacher, 85.

Games celebrated in the theatre at Jerusalem, 90.

Gardens of Gennesareth, 33.

Gath Hepher, the home of Jonah, 95.

Gaza, a Greek city, 70.

Gennesareth, the Plain of, a garden, 24.

size of, 33.

climate of, 33.

watered by a fine spring, 24.

origin and meaning of the name, 34.

wheat of, 33.

grain of, 39.

sugar-cane, 33.

peculiar character of, 33, 34.

tents on, for labourers, 33.

praised by Josephus, 22.

why its fruits not found at the feasts in Jerusalem, 25, 33.

Gennesareth, the Sea of, God's special delight, 28.

Gennesareth, the Sea of, how re-
    garded by the Christian, 28.
    see also Galilee, the Sea of.
Gergesa, on Wâdy Semakh, 50.
Gideon, pursuit of the Midianites,
    76.
Ginæa, Galileans attacked at, by the
    Samaritans, 78, 111
Gischala, an important city of Gali-
    lee, 54
    meaning of the name, 39
    production of oil, 38
    citizens of, wealthy, 99.
Gladiatorial contests at Cæsarea
    Philippi, 59
Glass-making near the river Belus,
    29.
Glass-shops of Tyre and Sidon, 42
Glass-vessels in common use, 42
    skill in manufacture of, 42
    price paid by Nero for one, 42.
Goats not profitable to raise in Gali-
    lee, 39.
God, belief in a personal, effect of
    on individual character, 71
Gold, vessels of, made in Sidon, 42.
Gophna reduced to slavery on ac-
    count of a tax by Cassius, 102
Gospel is for all the world, preached
    by Peter, 87.
Grain, production of, in different
    localities, 39, 40.
    stored in the towns of Galilee, 43
Grain and fruits raised in Galilee in
    preference to cattle, 25.
Grain merchants at Arabah, 40
Grapes of the Plain of Gennesareth,
    24, 39.
Greek influence not extensive in
    Christ's time, 70.
    in Galilee, 68.
Greek learning had a friend in
    Justus of Tiberias, 96.
Greeks in Tiberias a small fraction,
    70.
    numerous in Cæsarea, 70.
Grotto-sanctuary of Pan at Cæsarea
    Philippi, 55.
    described by Josephus, 56.

Hadrian, rebellion in Palestine
    under, 65
Hauran, the, full of ruined towns,
    66
Hazor, an important city of Galilee,
    54
    king of, defeated by Deborah and
    Barak, 76.
Hebrew spoken with purity in Ti-
    berias, 107.
    Jerome's teacher in, 107.
    Biblical, effort to maintain a
    knowledge of, in Christ's time,
    70
    scriptures the only school-book,
    85.
Hermon, Mount, eternal tent of
    snow, 56.
    dew of, 30.
Herod Agrippa I. appointed king
    of Trachonitis, &c , 13
    his wealth, 99.
    Cæsarea Philippi once governed
    by, 58.
    called king in Acts, 58
    persecuted the Christians, 13.
    beheaded James and arrested
    Peter, 13
    his death at Cæsarea on the sea-
    coast, 13, 58.
Herod Agrippa II. made king,
    13.
    heard Paul's defence at Cæsarea,
    14
    district governed by, 49
    besieged Gamala for seven
    months, 50
    is wounded there, 50.
    Cæsarea Philippi once governed
    by, 58.
    entertains Vespasian there, 59.
    service of, to the Romans in the
    Jewish war, 14, 75.
Herod Antipas, tetrarch of Peræa
    and Galilee, 12
    character as a ruler, 72
    neither lustful nor intemperate,
    90.
    palace of, at Tiberias, 99.

Herod Antipas, palace of, contained great treasures, 99.
  feeling aroused by his marrying Herodias, 88, 90.
  tried at Rome, 64.
  banished, 13.
  Galilee quiet and prosperous under, 79.
Herod the Great, governor of Galilee, 12, 110.
  the Galileans warmly attached to, 72.
  overcomes the robbers, 51, 77.
  declared king by the Roman Senate, 12.
  a good financier, 98.
  promptness in raising money for Cassius, 101.
  a generous provider for his family and kingdom, 98.
  makes liberal gifts, 98.
  adorns Paneas, 57.
  Cæsarea Philippi governed by, 58.
  Galilee quiet and prosperous during his reign, 79.
  found his best soldiers in Galilee, 72.
  had charge of the copper mines in Cyprus, 102.
  neither lustful nor intemperate, 90.
  plunged into a vessel of oil, 37.
  his death at Jericho, 12.
  his age, 12.
  lavish expense at his funeral, 99.
Herod Philip, tetrarch of Batanæa, Trachonitis, &c., 13.
  Cæsarea Philippi governed by, 58.
  rebuilds the Eastern Bethsaida, 50.
  builds his own tomb there, 50.
  enlarges Paneas, 57.
  his morals good, 90.
  a mild ruler, 79.
  his death, 13.
Herod, son of Gamalus, a prominent man in Tiberias, 96.

Herod, son of Miarus, a prominent man in Tiberias, 96.
Herodias divorced her husband Herod Philip (not the tetrarch), and caused thereby a great scandal, 88.
  married Herod Antipas, 13.
  loves her husband, 90.
  goes with him into exile, 90.
Hezekiah conquered by Sennacherib, 64.
Hezekiah, a brigand chief, 95.
Hillel not trained for a teacher, 84.
Hippocrates quoted, 33.
Hippos, 23.
  site of, 49.
  a Greek city, 70.
  merchants crossing the lake from, to Tiberias, 46.
History and locality to be studied in connection, 9.
Honey, Safed and Sepphoris celebrated for, 39, 40.
Hosea, the prophet, from Issachar, 95.
Houses, remarkable height of, in Zabulon, Tyre, Sidon, and Beirut, 54.
Huleh, plain and lake, 56.
  streams about the, numerous, 30.
Hyrcanus, John, sends his son Alexander Jannæus to Galilee to be brought up, 109.

Ibzan, a judge in Israel, from Zebulun, 94.
Ice-water in ancient times, 30.
  method of cooling water, 30.
Idumæa, Herod's old soldiers in, revolt at his death, 81.
Images and statues, sentiments of the Jews respecting, 88.
Indigo raised at Magdala, 40.
Industries of Galilee, 71.
Industry a characteristic of the Galileans, 71.
Inhabitants of Upper and Lower Galilee chiefly Jewish, 15, 16.

Iron mountain mentioned by Josephus, 102.
Italy, productions of, compared with those of Galilee, 25
   volunteers going from, to the Jewish war, 75.
Izates, court of, Eleazar a missionary at the, 91.

Jael, a heroine of Galilee, 94.
Jairus, a famous man of Galilee, 96.
James, son of Zebedee, 97.
   of Bethsaida, 51.
James, the brother of Christ, 97.
Japha, largest village in Galilee, 54, 74
   terrible fighting at, 74.
Jericho, method of cooling water at, 30
   Herod the Great dies at, 12, 38
   palace at, burned by Simon, 81.
Jerusalem, number of people in, at siege under Titus, 67.
   illustrated by recent investigations, 67.
   games like those of Italy and Greece celebrated in theatre at, 90.
Jewish prisoners compelled by Titus to destroy each other at Cæsarea Philippi, 59
Jewish learning flourished in Galilee subsequent to the time of Christ, 97.
Jews at Tiberias displeased with the luxury and Roman tastes of Antipas, 53
   exclusive in religion, 68, 69.
   noble treatment of strangers, 69.
   allowed foreigners to settle in Palestine, 69.
   at the time of Christ were settled in every country, 69
   everywhere a wealthy and influential class, 69, 98
   decrees of the Roman Senate in favour of, 69.
   cosmopolitan spirit of the, 69.

Jews surpassed the Greeks in numbers and wealth in Cæsarea, 98
   in Parthia and Arabia, 98.
   in Crete, Melos, and Rome, 98
   send vast sums from all parts of the world to the temple in Jerusalem, 98
   wronged by the Roman governors, 79
   by Felix, 80
   at last driven to madness, 80
Jezreel, a fertile region, 39.
   grain production of, 39
   an ancient battle-field, 76
John, of Bethsaida, 51.
   son of Zebedee, 97
John the Baptist had a strong party in Galilee, 91.
   Herod Antipas the murderer of, 52.
John of Gischala visits the warm springs of Tiberias, 31
   a shrewd man, 99
   monopolises the oil trade, 36, 37
   a person of wealth, 99
Jonah, from Zebulun, 95
Jordan, the, its upper and finer half belonged to Galilee, 29.
Joseph, the husband of Mary, 97.
Josephus, testimony of, as to the fertility of Galilee, 22
   of the Plain of Gennesareth, 24
   as to number of towns and inhabitants of Galilee, examined, 62–67
   has been misquoted, 63
   was military governor of Galilee, and knew its strength, 63.
   places fortified by, 63.
   was at Cana of Galilee, 60
   noble adherence of Galileans to, 72
   large army raised by, 63
Joshua fought a great battle near Lake Merom, 56.
Jotapata, forests about, 27.
   a strong city, 54
   fortified by Josephus, 54
   provisions in the siege of, 40.

Jotapata, heroic defence of by the Galileans, 60, 74.
boiling oil used against the Romans, 36.
its fall sealed the fate of Judæa, 74.
Judas, a celebrated teacher, 84.
Judas the Zealot, from Galilee, 77, 95.
founder of the sect of Galileans, 91.
a sterling puritan, 91.
the stubbornness of the Jewish resistance to Rome due largely to his influence, 91.
Judas, son of Hezekias, revolt of, on the death of Herod the Great, 81.
Judæa, how governed, from A.D. 7 to A.D. 66, 79.
Roman governors of, for the most part unprincipled men, 79.
condition of the country, 80.
priests and people become corrupt, 80.
its fields stony, 25.
common people in, poor and ignorant, 88.
exaggerated ideas of its wealth entertained at Rome, 99.
visited by foreigners for speculation and adventure, 99.
full of commotion during the long period when Galilee was quiet, 79.
Judæa and Galilee, contrast in the manner in which they were governed, 14.
no traces of sectional feeling between the inhabitants of, 112.
Judæans cared more for money than reputation, 89.
Judges of Israel that originated in Galilee, 94.
Julias, the Eastern Bethsaida called, 50.
mentioned by Pliny, 23.
Herod Philip buried in, 50.
Julius Severus sent to Palestine to crush the second rebellion, 65.

Justus, a prominent man in Tiberias, 96.
author of a history in Greek, 96.

Kadesh, an important city of Galilee, 54.
Kishon, a river of battle, 76.
belonged to Galilee, 29.

Labour, manual, how esteemed by the Galileans, 71.
by Christ, 119.
Christ practised and encouraged, 71.
Lake of Tiberias, beautiful, 23.
gliding waters, 22.
shores of, a garden, 23.
Lancashire, England, county of, inhabitants to a square mile, 20.
Landscapes in Galilee remarkably diversified, 22.
Languages, foreign, Jews' contempt for, 70.
at Pentecost, 108.
Law and order, Galileans' great respect for, 77.
Law of Moses, Galileans adhered to, in preference to tradition, 86.
Lebanon mountains, mineral deposits in the, 102.
Linen garments made in Bethshean, 39.
fabrics, women of Galilee celebrated for making, 40.
Litany, the, touches Galilee on the north, 29.
Looms of Sidon famous, 42.
Lydda reduced to slavery on account of tax by Cassius, 102.

Maccabees defend the Galileans, 111.
Magdala, 51.
the home of Mary Magdalene, 52.
pigeons sold at, for sacrifices, 40.
called the city of colour, 40.
sends treasures to Jerusalem, 100.
Malta, inhabitants of, to a square mile, 20.

Manahem, a famous man of Galilee, killed in Jerusalem, 95

Manufactured articles in Galilee, 38.

Maps of Galilee not correct, 17

Market, Phœnicia the great, of Galilee, 42, 43.

Market-places on the Sea of Galilee, 23

Marriage, laws respecting, sentiments concerning, 88

Mary, the mother of Christ, 97

Masada, slaughter at, 96.

Matthias, a celebrated teacher, 84

Megiddo, waters of, enter the Kishon, 29

Melos, Jews in, numerous and wealthy, 98.

Merchants, travelling, 100.

Merom, Lake, sweet water, 28.
  waters of, 56

Messiahs, false, people of Judæa easily led astray by, 92

Middlesex, England, county of, inhabitants to a square mile, 20.

Midianites pursued by Gideon, 76.

Mines of Judæa, 102.
  copper, 102
  gold, 102.
  lead, 102

Miracle of feeding the five thousand, scene of, 50

Mishna, several doctors of, from Galilee, 95.

Moab, expedition against, soon after time of Solomon, part taken by Galilee, 76.

Mœris, Lake, in Egypt, fisheries of, in ancient times, 45.
  large revenue from, 45.

Morals of the Galileans, 82.
  advantages over the people of Judæa, 82.

Moses, testimony of, respecting the richness of Galilee, 23.

Mountains, names and naming of, 115.

Nahum, the prophet, from Elkosh in Galilee, 95

Naphtali renowned for its fruits, 23.
  natural advantages of, 23.
  people of, brave, 76.

Nathanael, of Cana of Galilee, 96
  his words respecting Nazareth, 114.
  how best explained, 115.

Nazareth, 54.
  popular representations of, not correct, 10
  size and importance of, 113, et seq
  always called a city, 10.
  population of, 10, 116
  misrepresentations of, 105, 106, 113.
  no proof of immorality of, 114.
  not isolated, 117
  origin of the name, 114, et seq
  not mentioned in the Old Testament, 114
  hill behind, wonderful view from, 116.
  distances from, to certain points, 117.
  how regarded by the people of Jerusalem, 104–112.
  dialect of its inhabitants never referred to, 107.

Nero sold inhabitants of Tarichæa as slaves, 48.
  his canal at Corinth, 48.
  alarm of, at the magnitude of revolt in Judæa, 73

News, early, Nazareth favourably situated to receive, 117.

Nitai, eminent doctor of the Mishna, from Arbela, 95.

Oil furnished by Solomon to Hiram, 37.
  Galilee furnished, to Phœnicia, 43
  production of, 35

Oil, article of commerce, 35.
  a source of wealth, 36.
  trouble about pure, at Cæsarea Philippi, 36
  boiling, used in defending Jotapata, 36.

Oil, quantity stored in the towns of Upper Galilee, 36.
  peculiar kind of jars needed for preserving, 40, 41.
  Herod the Great plunged into a vessel of, 37.
  used in sickness, 37, 38.
  such use commended by Christ, 37, 38.
Olive trees easily raised in Galilee, 35.
  of the Plain of Gennesareth, 22.
  of Bethshean, 39.

Palestine, number of square miles in, 19.
  in Eastern, 20.
  in Western, 20.
  how governed from B.C. 47 to A.D. 66, 12-14.
Palms of the Plain of Gennesareth, 24.
  in Galilee, 25.
Pan, grotto-sanctuary of, at Cæsarea Philippi, 56.
Paneas, 55.
  various names of, 55.
  supposed birthplace of Alexander, a Jewish philosopher of Alexandria, 95.
Paradise, Bethshean, the 'gate of, 39.
Parthia, Jews in, 98.
Parthians invade Palestine, 12.
  reach Jerusalem, 12.
  take Phasaëlus, a brother of Herod the Great, prisoner, 12.
Patriotism, Galileans noted for, 71, 72.
Patronius, treatment of the Jews by, 80.
Paul, the apostle, tradition that he came from Gischala, 96.
Peræa, a portion of, possibly belonged to Galilee, 19.
  multitude of towns in, 66.
  Simon incites a rebellion in, on the death of Herod the Great, 81.

Peter from Bethsaida, 51.
  representative man of Galilee, 97.
  vision of, at Joppa, 87.
  speech or dialect of, 108, 109.
Pharisees rose to power in reign of Alexandra, 83.
Phasaëlus, military governor of Judæa, 12.
  taken prisoner by the Parthians, and kills himself, 12.
Pheasants, Achabara celebrated for, 39.
Philip, from Bethsaida, 51, 97.
Philip, Herod, see Herod.
Philo quoted respecting the synagogues being schools of piety, 85.
Phœnicia, influence of, on Galilee, 41, 42, 43, 68.
  mariners of, bringing news to Syria, 41.
Phœnician coast once covered with towns, 66.
Phœnicians, glass manufactories of, 29, 42.
  surpasses other nations in the matter of shipping, 43.
  connecting link between the East and West, 41.
  receive oil and other supplies from Galilee, 35, 36, 37.
Physicians of Herod the Great, 37.
Pigeons for sacrifices sold at Magdala, 40.
Pilate, treatment of the Jews by, 80.
Pistus, a prominent man of Tiberias, 96.
Pliny, on the warm springs of Tiberias, 31.
  on the towns about the Lake of Gennesareth, 23.
Ploughmen turning a furrow with skill, 25.
Poetry, talent for, finely developed among the Galileans, 93.
  scenery and climate foster the spirit of, 93.

Pomegranates flourish at Shikmonah, 39.
Population of Galilee, 20
Pottery, vessels of, for preserving oil, 40, 41.
  great variety of, 41.
  black, most highly prized, 41.
Preaching, severe, of Judas and Eleazar, 91.
Priesthood, how degraded in Jerusalem, 87.
Priests become corrupt, 80.
  poorer priests suffer, 80.
Productions of Galilee, agricultural and manufactured, 35–45.
  of the Plain of Gennesareth, 24.
  furnished to Phœnicia by Galilee, 43.
  the present, of Galilee, 27.
Prophets from Galilee, 94, 95, 110.
  their memory cherished, 94, 95.
Ptolemais, Roman army massed at, previous to entering Galilee, 71.
Ptolemy Epiphanes, his general, Scopas, defeated at Paneas, 56.

Rabbis, testimony of, as to the Lake of Tiberias, 22.
  the towns on the shores, 23
  the land of Naphtali, 23.
  not allowed to receive pay for instruction, 84.
Ramah, important town in Galilee, 54.
Religion, in matters of, Jews allowed no interference, 69.
  exclusiveness in, 69.
  among the Galileans, 82
  advantage of the latter over the people of Judæa, 83
Renan, praise of Galilee, 23
Research, Galilee a rich field for, 18.
Revelation, a divine, implies history, 9.

Rimmon, important town in Galilee, 54
Road from Southern Galilee to Damascus, 52.
  infested by robbers near Arbela, 51
  east from Paneas, 57.
  width of, 57
  from Paneas to Tyre, 57.
  to Sidon, 57
  guarded by castles, 57.
  caravan routes through Galilee, 118.
  routes of commerce, 100
Robbers in the caves of Arbela subdued by Herod the Great, 51, 78.
Roman emperor, grain tribute of, in Galilee, 40
  governors of Judæa, in distinction from Galilee, corrupt men, 79
  rob and oppress the Jews, 79.
  countenance bribery and lawlessness, 80.
  conduct of Felix, Florus, Sabinius, Patronius, Pilate, 80.
  troops of Sabinius, attack upon, in Jerusalem, 112.
  Senate, decrees of, in favour of the Jews, 69
Romans suffer in siege of Jotapata, 36
Rome, financial crisis in, affecting Palestine, 80
  Jews in, numerous and wealthy, 98
Rulers, loyalty of Galileans to, 72.
Ruined towns in the region near Hamah, 66
  in Bashan, 66

Sabinius, treatment of the Jews by, 80
  Roman troops of, attacked in Jerusalem, 112.
Sacrifices, pigeons for, sold at Magdala, 40.

Safed, lofty situation, 54, 55.
  one of the sacred cities of the
    Jews, 55.
  fertile region about, 39.
  celebrated for its honey, 39.
Sailors formed a large class in Tibe-
    rias, 53.
Salome, the wife of Zebedee, 97.
Samaritans lay south of Galilee,
    68.
  influence upon the Galileans, 68.
  once attack the latter, at Ginæa,
    78, 111.
  friendly intercourse between the,
    and the Galileans, 79.
Sanhedrin, dominant influence of,
    in Jerusalem, 86.
Scenery of Galilee, 93.
  about Banias, 56.
Schools, Jewish, connected with
    synagogues, 85.
  method of instruction in, 85.
  school system, 84.
  alleged that the Galileans had
    none, 83.
Schools not colleges or seminaries,
    in the modern meaning of these
    terms, 84.
Schools and learned men, friendly
    intercourse between those of
    Galilee and Judæa, 86.
School system, rabbinical, too great
    antiquity ascribed to, 84.
Scopas defeated near Paneas, 56.
Scythopolis belonged to Galilee, 61.
  largest city of Decapolis, 61.
  population of, 54.
  Syrians in, 70.
  winters the Fifteenth Legion, 61,
    100.
Seas, Jews say that seven were
    created, 28.
  names of the, 28.
Sects in Jerusalem, cheerless atmo-
    sphere among, 87.
Semakh, Wâdy, Gergesa situated
    on, 50.
Semechonitis, one of the seven seas,
    28.

Sennacherib, invasion of Palestine
    by, 64.
Sepphoris, capital of Galilee, 53.
  in a fertile region, 23.
  citizens of, wealthy, 99.
  archives of the province kept in,
    55.
  celebrated for grain and fruit, 39.
  royal arsenal at, 55.
  seat of one of Gabinius' five coun-
    cils, 61.
  feeling between its inhabitants
    and those of Tiberias, 53.
  taken by Judas after the death of
    Herod the Great, 81, 95.
  degraded below Tiberias, and
    again elevated above it, 53.
  near Nazareth, 118.
Sermon on the Mount, what it pre-
    supposes on the part of the
    listeners, 91.
  could not have been preached in
    Judæa, 91.
Sheep, not profitable to raise, in
    Galilee, 39.
Shihor Libnath perhaps identical
    with the river Belus, 29.
Shikmonah, pomegranates of, 39.
Ships and boats on the Sea of Gali-
    lee, 46, 47.
Ship-building at Tarichæa, 49.
Shipping, Phœnicians surpass other
    nations in, 43.
Sicarii committed their worst crimes
    in Judæa, 79.
  originated in Jerusalem, 81.
  meaning of the name, 81.
Sichin, manufacturer of pottery at,
    40.
  sends treasures to Jerusalem,
    100.
Sidon, lofty houses in, 54.
  brass shops of, 42.
  gold and silver vessels of, 42.
  glass shops, 42.
  road leading from Damascus and
    Cæsarea Philippi to, 57.
Signalling, means for, from point to
    point, 58.

Sigona, wine production of, 39.

Sikars, see Sicarii.

Silas, governor of Tiberias, 96.

Silver, vessels of, made in Sidon, 42.

Simon incites a rebellion in Peræa, on the death of Herod the Great, 81.

burns the palace in Jericho, 81.

Simon, a famous man of Galilee, 95

Sinaitic peninsula, gold deposits in, 102.

Sisera routed by Deborah and Barak, 76.

Slavery, cities reduced to, on account of tax levied by Cassius, 102.

Snow on Hermon, cools the air, 30.

used as a luxury in the large cities, 30.

also by labourers, 30.

Biblical references to the use of, 30.

Sodom, Sea of, one of seven seas, 28.

Sohemus aids the Romans in the Jewish war, 75

Soil of Galilee, fertility of the, 25.

Solomon gives twenty cities to Hiram, 15

importance of these places, 16.

provisions furnished to Hiram by, 37.

supplies furnished for palace of, by Galilee, 27.

Song of Solomon thought by some to have originated in Galilee, 23, 93.

Song of Deborah originated in Galilee, 93

Spade, fields cultivated with the, in Galilee, 25.

Springs abundant in Galilee, 30.

Statues and images, sentiments of the Jews respecting, 88.

Stones, precious, art of engraving in early times at Tyre and Sidon, 42.

Strabo quoted, 33.

mentions the inhabitants of Galilee, 16.

on the colonies of Tyre, 41.

on the height of houses in Tyre and Sidon, 54.

on the wealth of the Jews, 98.

Strangers allowed to settle in Palestine, 69.

treated in a noble manner by the Jews, 69

Sugar-cane on the Plain of Gennesareth, 33.

Sycamores not found in Upper Galilee, 19.

flourished in Lower Galilee, 19.

Synagogues, elegant, at Tiberias, 53.

number of, 85

existed in every city and important town, 85.

this confirmed by the words of Christ, 86.

schools connected with, 85

worship in, strictly maintained in Galilee, 87.

Syria full of ruined towns, 66.

Syrians lay north of Galilee, 68.

influence of, on the Galileans, 68.

honour Herod the Great for his victory over the robbers, 78.

in Scythopolis, 70.

numerous in Cæsarea on the seacoast, 70.

supplied with oil from Galilee, 35, 38.

Tabor, Mount, a stronghold, 54.

taken by Antiochus the Great, 54.

Alexander, son of Aristobulus, defeated at, 55.

Deborah and Barak rallied their forces at, 76.

River Kishon rises near the foot of, 29.

Talmud, that of Jerusalem preferable to that of Babylon for matters relating to Palestine, 106.

Talmud, evidence of, 39.
Tarichæa, 23.
 situation of, 48.
 population of, 54.
 foreigners there, 70.
 numerous ships at, 46.
 bloody sea-fight at, 46.
 inhabitants of, sold as slaves by Nero, 48.
 also by Cassius, 48.
 Josephus taken there when wounded, 49.
 larger than Tiberias, 49.
 importance of, as compared with Tiberias, 70.
 fish business of, 43.
 fish factories, 44.
 name derived from this industry, 43.
 ship-building at, 49.
Teachers, qualification of, 84.
 the most eminent were found in Jerusalem, 86.
 eminent ones in Sepphoris and Tiberias, 85.
Tekoa, production of oil at, 35.
Temple at Jerusalem robbed by Crassus of a large amount of gold and silver, 98.
Tents of Gennesareth, for labourers and others, 33.
Thamna reduced to slavery on account of a tax, 102.
Theatre at Jerusalem, 90.
Tiberias, 23.
 situation and importance of, 52.
 Herod Antipas beautifies it, 52.
 his costly buildings at, 52.
 when the city was built, 53.
 old burying-ground found at, 53.
 hence unclean to the Jews, 53.
 this prejudice overcome, 53.
 warm springs of, 31.
 a resort for health and pleasure, 32.
 people attracted to it, 32.
 a racecourse at, 90.
 synagogue built by Antipas, 53.
 number of synagogues at, 85.

Tiberias, degraded below Sepphoris, in time of Agrippa II., 53.
 fortified by Josephus, 53.
 unfriendly to him, 49.
 ·Vespasian requires three legions to attack it, 53.
 council of, 53.
 did Christ ever visit it ? 53.
 one of the sacred cities of the Jews, 55.
 Greeks in, a small fraction of the inhabitants, 70.
 treasure in the palace of Antipas, 99.
 ancient method of cooling water at, 30.
 Jerome obtained a Hebrew teacher from, 107.
 conduct of inhabitants of, with regard to Caius' setting up his statue in the temple, 88.
Tiberias, Lake of, highly praised by the Jews, 28.
 merchants crossing the, from Tiberias to Hippos, 46.
Tiberius Alexander, Cæsarea Philippi once governed by, 58.
Tiglath Pileser, invasion of Galilee by, 56.
Timber in Galilee, 23.
 furnished the Phœnicians, for ships, 43.
Titus with Vespasian at Cæsarea Philippi, 59.
 later, he exhibits games there, 59.
 cruelties to the Jewish prisoners at, 59.
 praises the conduct of the Galileans in the war, 75.
Tobacco cultivated in Galilee, 27.
Tobit, from Naphtali, 95.
 interesting account of his home and times, 95.
Tola, a judge from Issachar, 94.
Towns of Galilee, see Cities and towns.
Tradition adhered to in Jerusalem in preference to the law of Moses, 86.

Tradition, charge that the Galileans neglected, 86.

Traditional sites conflict with the results of modern researches, 18.

Traffic, inland, through Galilee, 100.

Transfiguration, scene of, near Cæsarea Philippi, 59.

Transportation an important industry of Galilee, 71.

Trees, what, flourished in Galilee, 26

retain foliage throughout the year on the Plain of Gennesareth, 33.

Tribes which settled in Galilee in Joshua's time, 64

Towns fortified by Josephus in Galilee, 63

Tyre, colonies and commerce of, 41.
purple dye of, 41
this is a source of wealth, 42.
glass shops of, 42
its fine houses, 54.
number of stories in some, 54.
road leading to, from Damascus and Banias, 57.

Vespasian sent to command the Roman army in the Jewish war, 73
besieges Gamala with three legions, 50
nearly loses his life, 50.
approaches Tiberias with three legions, 53.
takes and burns Gadara, 60
massacres the inhabitants, 60.
besieges Jotapata, 60.
rests his army at Cæsarea Philippi, 59.
celebrates his victory over the Galileans, 59.
praises their conduct, 75.
recruits his army, 75.
his troops winter at Scythopolis, 100.

Villages and cities of Galilee, see Cities and villages.

Vitellius favours the Jews, 81.

War, second Jewish, in time of Hadrian, terrible slaughter on both sides, 65

Warm springs of Galilee, 31.
opposite Jericho, visited by Herod the Great, 37.

Water, cold, provided for travellers and the sick, 31.

Water-brooks abound in Galilee, 23

Watercourses, ancient, remains of, 32

Watering-place, ancient, at the hot springs of Tiberias, 31.

Weaving at Tyre and Sidon, 42

Wheat in Northern Galilee, 39
of Chorazin and Capernaum, 39.
of the Plain of Gennesareth, 33
furnished by Galilee to Phœnicia, 43
furnished by Solomon to Hiram, 37

Widow of a deceased brother, custom about marrying, 88.

Wine, production of, at Sigona, 39
furnished by Galilee to Phœnicia, 43.
furnished by Solomon to Hiram, 37.

Women of Galilee celebrated for making linen fabrics, 40

Woollen cloth made at Magdala, 40.

Zabulon, a beautiful city, 54
houses of, modelled after those of Tyre, 54.

Zebedee, of Bethsaida, 51
a man of means, 97, 100.

Zebulun and Naphtali, bravery of the people of, 76

Zeller, Rev. Dr., of Nazareth, testimony of, as to the fertility of Galilee, 26

Zenodorus, Cæsarea Philippi once belonged to, 58

Milton Keynes UK
Ingram Content Group UK Ltd.
UKHW022024110923
428497UK00005B/115